# DRINK SMALL

## The Life & Music of South Carolina's Blues Doctor

Gail Wilson-Giarratano, PhD

The History Press

Published by The History Press
Charleston, SC 29403
www.historypress.net




*Back cover images*: Courtesy of the *Charlotte Observer*.

First published 2014

Manufactured in the United States

ISBN 978.1.62619.740.4

Library of Congress Control Number: 2014953164

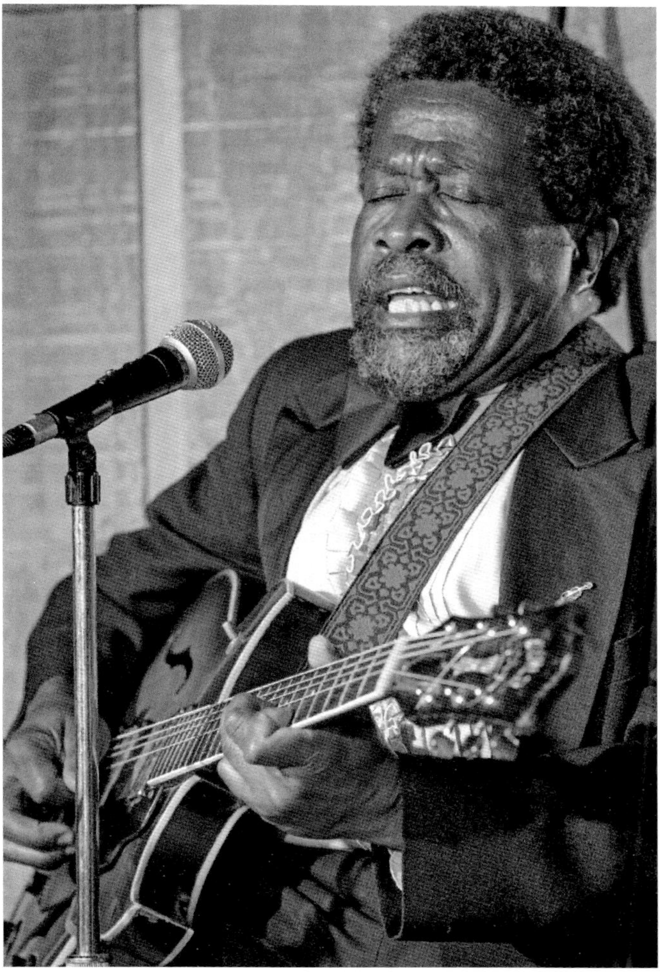

February 18, 1990 feature story by Elizabeth Lealand, Bob Leverone photographer. *Courtesy of the* Charlotte Observer.

*The blues is not something that I do. It something that in me.*
*—Drink Small*

# CONTENTS

# FOREWORD

Currently in the blues realm, there is a disturbing tendency to apply the term "legend" to practically anyone who has stepped onto the stage, sung into a microphone and played an instrument for as brief as a couple of years. Make no mistake about it—South Carolina's native son Drink Small is a legend in the truest sense of the word.

Although I only vaguely recall it, Drink Small reminds me that he and I first met some twenty years ago in Charleston, South Carolina, when I was doing a series of Blues in Schools residencies that ultimately evolved into the Charleston Blues Festival, which had that name from 1991 to 1993. Due to the efforts of Carolina musician/promoter Gary Erwin, the festival continued under the name Lowcountry Blues Bash for another nineteen years. The fact that he remembers that brief encounter in detail (he has described it to me on several occasions) is a demonstration of his incredible memory and provides a brief glimpse into the psyche of this remarkable octogenarian.

As a professional musician for more than sixty years, Drink is exceptional and unique. He is a rare musical talent whose repertoire includes multiple genres and styles, including gospel, Piedmont blues, Chicago blues, rhythm and blues and funk. He is the "Blues Doctor." His original songs attest to that, from the serious to the comically absurd and downright dirty, always thoughtful, entertaining, always Drink.

"America Will Never Be the Same" is a heartfelt homage to President Barack Obama. "If You Tell One Lie You Got to Tell Another" and "Too

Much Water (You Don't Have to Be Funky)" exemplify his folksy wit. "Tittie Man" and "Leave Your Panties Home" show Drink's humorous, "dirty" side.

As recently as three years ago, for the second time, I had the pleasure of having Drink as my guest instructor during a two-week residency of my Blues in Schools program in Columbia, South Carolina. Drink's homespun anecdotes and warm southern charm proved to be the perfect bait to hook these adolescent high school students. It is noteworthy to mention that in both instances, these were African American youngsters who, like their parents and peers, were at first reluctant to embrace the blues, although the blues are, without a doubt, their cultural heritage.

However, Drink possesses an ace in the hole that never fails to win over even the most reticent of audiences: his "Drinkisms."

According to Drink: "What is Drinkism? The way Drink thinks. What gives him the decision to make Drinkism? How you know you got it? Take some of Drink's knowledge, and put a little wisdom, add a little rhythm and you got the Drinkism."

A few Drinkisms:

"A lot of people get confused by the blues."

"You can have money and no honey."

"You can be rich and ain't got no sense. You just a rich fool."

"I ain't rich, but I got sense." (He does not neglect to point out that "cents" and "sense" are homonyms.)

Drink Small is the consummate storyteller/philosopher. He often expresses his insights in the form of rhyme: "We had forty-three presidents before, all of them white. The Lord gave us a black president because he knew it wasn't right." "If I was white they'd call it bluegrass, but 'cause I'm black they call it nut grass."

These lighthearted utterances belie a highly analytical intellect. Over the years during our many conversations, Drink has shared with me his thoughtful views on politics, race, music and religion, as well as various other topics. "In the computer world you can go online, you can learn and sit on your behind." "It takes a guy like me forty years to learn what you can now learn in two hours."

He feels that the current musical trends exclude the older musicians in favor of younger artists: "What makes me so mad when it comes to the blues is that Beethoven died hundreds of years ago and his music is still revered. They take the blues and just throw it around. Folks come and 'invent' stuff that was already around. You got to go a thousand miles to find something good, and you had it here all the time.

"The blues didn't begin in the South; it started in Africa. Those slaves didn't want to come here; they made them come."

Take it from me: this brother is as sharp as a razor blade. One of Drink's more notable awards includes the South Carolina Folk Heritage Award (1990), and in 1999, he was inducted into the South Carolina Hall of Fame. Like so many other legendary bluesmen, fame and financial success have eluded him. He is not bitter but somewhat saddened by the lack of opportunities to perform. Though Drink Small has lost his eyesight, his talent has not diminished. This effervescent, gentle soul is still adept, capable and eager to perform his thoroughly original and entertaining songs while captivating you with his inexhaustible supply of Drinkisms. I sincerely hope that he is afforded every opportunity to do so. He deserves that much, and actually, so do we.

BILLY BRANCH
Winner of the prestigious Emmy Award, Addy Award and multiple Handy (Blues Foundation) Awards, three-time Grammy nominee, founder of the Grammy Blues Committee and a retired governor for the Chicago Grammy Chapter of NARAS
*August 3, 2014*

# ACKNOWLEDGEMENTS

I'd like to thank everyone who provided information, support, feedback, guidance and inspiration for this project. Special thanks to Billy Branch; Scott Deridder, Columbia Print and Graphics; the Cultural Council of Richland and Lexington County; Clair DeLune; Gary Erwin; the Finnish Blues Society; Robyn Ford; Cassie J. Fox; Elfi Hacker and the 145 Club; Catherine Townes Johnson, Esquire; Kari Kempas; Bernd Kreikmann; Bob Leverone; Sam McCuen; Victor Perlin; Wasser Prawda; Heather Siegfried; Andrina Bratton Small; and the South Carolina Arts Commission. I extend my deep appreciation to Dr. Rhondda Robinson Thomas for her years of friendship and months of technical support. I am grateful to my family, Marvin and Harriett Wilson, Kitty and John Evans, Vanessa, Rob and Pepper Wilson-Maurice. Finally, to my loving husband, Anthony Charles (Giarratano), thank you not only for your support but also, if you had not added the blues harmonica to your arsenal of musical talents, I might never have reconnected with Drink Small. Special love to Adelina Bambina, R.A.G. and Sergio forever.

This book required a group of special individuals to take a leap of faith and kick-start our efforts. Thanks to all who supported the early campaign and especially those who stepped up to be called "Friends of Drink Small."

Alice K. Adams
Ricky and Debbie Broom
Jimmy Burroughs
Malcolm Calder
Anthony Charles
Steve Douglas
Linda McLaughlin Dye
Dan Freeman
John and Cheryl Hartness
Philip Hedgecock
Mary Henderson
Vince Jackson
Heather Jones
Steve Jones
Bernrd Kreikmann
Brian LaPrade
The Majidy family
Edward Manning II
Tonja Koob Marking
Robert Maurice
John D. Peterson
D. Lindsay Pettus
Stephen Rose
Strauss Moore Shiple
Robert Vanderwege
Vanessa Wilson
Kitty Wilson-Evans
RD Peppy Winchel Jr.

# INTRODUCTION

Drink Small and I first met in the late 1980s through our work with the South Carolina Arts Commission. I was working for the Lancaster County Council for the Arts, attending the University of South Carolina at Lancaster and performing in South Carolina schools as a storyteller for the commission's Arts in Education program. Drink Small was the Columbia-based well-known "Blues Doctor," a South Carolina legend.

Today, Drink has far fewer moments on stage with his guitar, Geraldine; however, his fans remain as loyal as they were when they first heard him on their college campuses, at gospel music caravans, at blues festivals or private parties, nightclubs or other major venues. Original songs such as "Bishopville Is My Hometown" and "Shag My Blues Away" immediately bring back memories for thousands of adults throughout the region and beyond. You can travel from the Lowcountry and Pee Dee to the Piedmont region and find more than enough individuals happy to share their most cherished Drink Small story, favorite song or Drinkism. Although individuals quickly recognize his signature bass voice, few know much about his personal story. I certainly didn't.

After working for the Lancaster Arts Council, I continued pursuing a career in theater while working at the Museum of York County and completing my undergraduate studies at Winthrop University. I left South Carolina in 1989 for New York City, and twenty-four years later, I returned home and reconnected with Drink Small at his eightieth birthday party. He was now totally blind but still playing the blues. That birthday celebration was one I shall never forget.

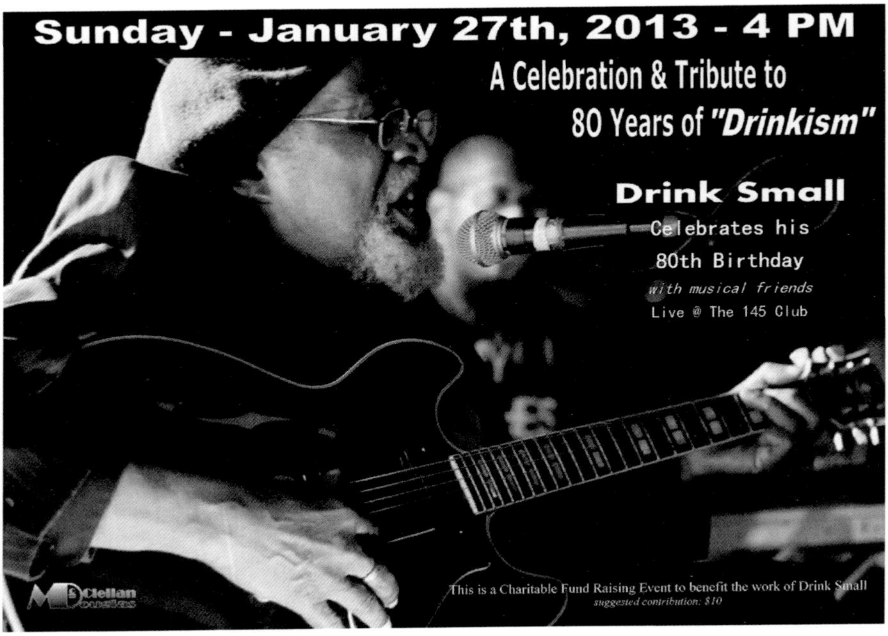


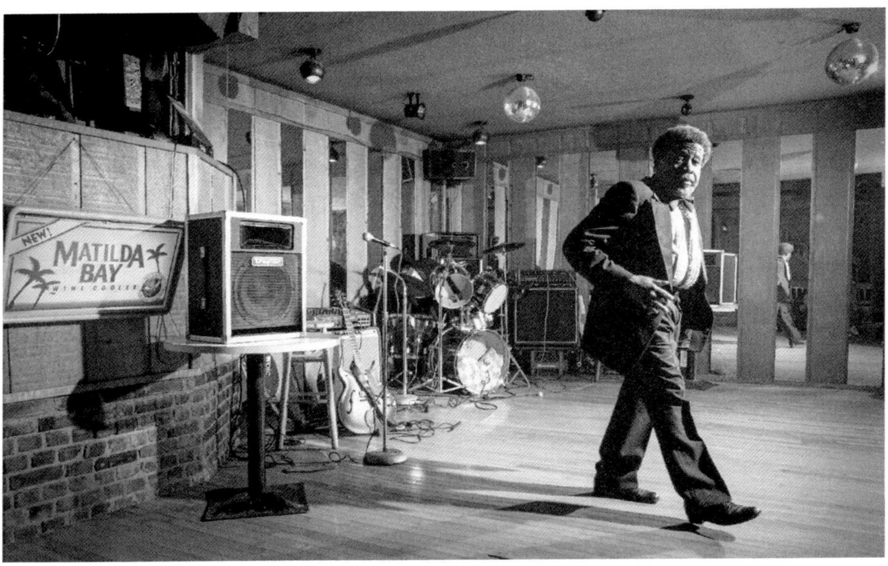


February 18, 1990 feature story by Elizabeth Lealand, Bob Leverone photographer. *Courtesy of the* Charlotte Observer.

On a chilly winter Sunday, January 27, 2013, at 4:00 p.m. in Winnsboro, South Carolina, the 145 Club hosted "A Celebration and Tribute to 80 Years of 'Drinkism.'" Drink Small's birthday blues bash was planned by Elfi Hacker, the club's owner. By 3:00 p.m., both sides of South Congress Street were lined with cars. The news had gone out—word of mouth, radio, newspaper, Facebook, e-mail, Twitter, phone calls, event calendars and announcements at jam sessions from the hills of the Upcountry to the palmetto-lined streets of the Lowcountry. On the afternoon of the event, a young television camerawoman was setting up equipment outside and a reporter from the *Harold Independent* was already jotting down quotes in her notebook from the quickly forming crowd that consisted of musicians, blues lovers, well-wishers and friends, old and new. Jimmy Burroughs, retired police chief and director of Christ Central Ministries, was quoted as saying, "I have known Drink since the '70s, when he played on my radio show at WCKM. I enjoy spending as much time with him as possible playing the guitar at home with him. He is the last of the true blues artists in America." My husband, Anthony Charles, was then serving as president of the Midlands Blues Society and one of the event organizers. At 4:30 p.m., a driver pulled Drink's white van up to the curb, and members of his devoted group of musicians hopped out and got to work. It was a well-choreographed procession, a familiar routine. Those assigned to unload the instruments, music stands and CDs carefully did so and made a direct path inside. Drink was looking sharp and ready for his grand entrance. To shield himself from the cold, he pulled a black beret down over his ears just as the young camerawoman called out, "Sir? Can I get a shot before you head inside?" He was standing almost directly next to the black-and-white poster in the window that displayed an image of him playing the guitar. Drink thrust his hands deep in the pockets of his trench coat and looked straight ahead without a smile. He struck a surly pose for the young photographer like he had done hundreds of times before.

A week after the party, we were visiting Drink and his wife, Andrina (Drina), in their home in Columbia on Truman Street. At some point, Drina leaned over to me and said, "We want you to write a book on Drink." I was shocked. I tried to explain that I was not that kind of writer. Drink looked in the direction of my voice and said, "You're a storyteller, ain't you? I just want my story told. I ain't got a lot of time."

# PART I

# BISHOPVILLE IS MY HOMETOWN

## *Chapter 1*

# I KNOW MY BLUES ARE DIFFERENT

Drink Small fell facedown in the dirt, the upper portion of his small body lodged directly in front of the shifting wheel of the wagon. Before he could cry out for help or crawl from beneath the wagon wheel, he found himself pinned on the ground in unspeakable pain. Drink rarely discusses the terrible accident that took place near the cotton fields when he was about eight years old. The cotton fields were part of the Stuckey family farm in Bishopville, South Carolina, that was originally a cotton plantation. The Smalls, along with approximately fifty other African American families, lived and worked on the farm as sharecroppers.

Annie Lou Moses was eighteen years old at the time and had been picking cotton with her mother and father the day the accident occurred. She recalls seeing Drink riding in the wagon with his uncle, Louis Small, who was driving the gray mule that pulled the wagon along the narrow path next to the rows of cotton. Drink hated picking cotton and often begged his mother, Alice Small (nicknamed Missy), to allow him to ride in the wagon instead. Louis sat on a narrow makeshift bench attached to the front of the wagon so he could control the mule. He stopped the wagon at predetermined spots, retrieved sacks filled with cotton from each family member and emptied the large sacks into the wagon bed.

The accident must have occurred about midday because the wagon was already piled with cotton that Drink's grandmother, mother, uncles and aunts had picked for the past five or six hours. The wagon wheel suddenly dropped into a trench along the side of the road and jolted the wagon sideways.

Louis tried to keep the startled mule moving forward, but the wheel was stuck in the narrow ditch. As the mule pulled, the wagon jerked violently and sent a great deal of cotton and the little boy over the side rail. Louis, completely unaware of what had happened, continued to slap the reins. The mule heaved and stomped, and suddenly, the wagon lurched forward. Annie Lou recalls, "[Drink] jus' fell out, and next thing the wagon wheel rolled right over him."

Drink's mother, Missy, and his grandmother Emma Bishop Small had been walking toward the pickup spot with their cotton sacks. As soon as they realized what had happened, the women began screaming. Louis jumped out of the wagon and called for his brother, Joseph "Joe" Small, to help. Annie Lou's father, Deacon Matthew Moses, stopped picking cotton as soon as he heard the screams, dropped his cotton sack and ran across the dirt road to the Jerusalem Stuckey Baptist Church. Dr. Stuckey, the patriarch of the prominent family, had built the church for the sharecroppers. Deacon Moses frantically rang the cast-iron bell located near the church doors to notify everyone that something very serious had happened.

As Joseph took control of the mule wagon, Drink's grandmother Emma began gathering the cotton that had fallen along the road. Louis carried Drink toward the row of tiny wood-frame houses located behind the church while Missy ran alongside her crying child. Once they reached their house, there was not much that could be done. Louis and Missy could not leave the farm to get help for Drink because lost time equaled lost wages. Missy put a cloth over the floorboards while Louis gently laid down the child. Upon impact, Drink wailed, cried and passed out. Louis and Missy reluctantly returned to the cotton field to complete the day's work.

The midwife, a sharecropper on a neighboring farm, came by the Smalls' house shortly after the accident. For the poor sharecroppers, the midwife delivered babies, cared for mothers during more complicated pregnancies and provided emergency medical care on occasions. Drink does not remember her name, but he does remember that she had to be paid for her services. His family only called her for a life-and-death emergency. The midwife did not stay long; she examined Drink's swollen torso and wound. He does not recall what the midwife told his mother to do, but shortly after she left, Missy took a bucket outside and returned with a thick mud-clay mixture. Missy gently applied the mixture on Drink's back and tightly wrapped his body with thin strips of flannel and wool. As the clay dried, the fabric bandages created a firm, heavy body cast that made it difficult for Drink to lie down. He found it more comfortable to kneel in front of a small wooden milk stool and bend forward to rest his stomach on the seat and easily use his arms and hands. Drink stayed in this position for hours and even slept this way while his relatives worked in the cotton field. His mother positioned the family radio on the floor so he could reach it. He spent the days listening to WAGS, Bishopville's country radio station that featured music from the Grand Ole Opry. Drink never grew tired of listening to songs like "The Louisiana Hayride" and Hank Williams playing the guitar. The radio was more than a way to pass time; it became Drink Small's entire world.

Approximately three or four weeks passed before the midwife returned to help Missy cut off the hard fabric strips. Missy washed the clay off Drink's skin and scrubbed him down with brine, helping the wound to heal. Drink never regained enough strength to return to cotton picking on a regular basis. He performed less strenuous chores on the farm and attended the Jerusalem Stuckey School that Dr. Stuckey had built along with the church. Thinking back on those days, Drink says, "I was lucky I didn't have to pick much cotton. That's why I say—I was ah—lucky."

The Small family had lived and worked in Lee County for four generations. The region was named after General Robert E. Lee and was formed from parts of Sumter, Kershaw and Darlington Counties in 1902. The particular tract of land the Smalls always considered home was originally known as Singleton's Crossroads and included some of the richest soil in South Carolina. The Singleton family, one of several prominent families in that area, had established large plantations that relied on slave labor. Eventually, the Singleton family sold the property to Dr. Jacques Bishop, and by 1830, the settlement was officially renamed Bishopville.

Bishopville, located in the heart of Lee County, eventually became the county seat. By the late 1800s, Lee County (although the smallest county in the state) was the largest producer of cotton. Slave labor, primarily planting, picking and harvesting the crop, was critical for the region's economic success. Over time, land and slaves were sold from one family to another.

Early census records provide insights into Drink's ancestry, but records can be challenging to understand because of the institution of slavery and misrepresentation of names and ages on census documents. For example, Drink's grandmother Emma Bishop (Small) was likely born in Sumter County in the mid-1800s. The 1870 Sumter County census for the Carters Crossing Township lists a fourteen-year-old black female, Emma Bishop, as a farm laborer. It could be possible that the fourteen-year-old was Drink's great-grandmother, as it was customary to name children after their parents, who were often given the surname of their master. However, Emma Small, wife of Oma Small, was listed in the Lee County 1910 census as being the black thirty-two-year-old mother of four living children. This would put Emma's birth in 1878, after slavery was abolished when the Civil War ended in 1865.

Emma Small's likely hometown, Carters Crossing, is located in Sumter County. Another wealthy landowner, James Ellis Stuckey, also called "Captain Jim," resided in the township of Carters Crossing and owned most of the land south of what is now Bishopville. Captain James bequeathed parcels of land to his children, including five children he fathered with Laura (Nellie) Slater, his African American cook and housekeeper. Although South Carolina miscegenation laws prohibited Captain Jim from marrying Nellie Slater, they did not prohibit him from acknowledging his mixed-race children as his own. He even wanted them to call him "daddy," according to family history provided by Demetrius DeBerry, an African American descendant.

At some point, Emma Bishop Small moved to the Fannie Davis farm located outside the town of Bishopville. Drink has no knowledge of the exact date or conditions associated with these events. Drink stated that Emma Bishop met Oma Small, his grandfather, on the Stuckey farm. He explains, "I don't know when my grandmother was born, but she died in 1946 or '47...You gonna give me a stroke asking me to think back that far...She was born on a farm owned by the Bishop brothers. That's where she married my grandfather Oma [Small]...I can't tell you no more than that—I'm 80, not 180!" The couple had eight children. According to Drink, the boys included Pickett, Oma Jr., Louis and Joseph. The girls were Sarah; his mother, Alice, known as Missy; Hattie, known as Noon; and Carrie. Although Drink stated that he cannot recall the birth order for all the children, he does know that Sarah was the oldest child, Joseph was the baby and all of them had to work. The 1910 census confirms that Emma (age thirty-two) and Oma (age thirty-five) were married. Their children at that time included Sarah (age nine), Pickett (age seven), Anna (actually Alice, Drink's mother, age six) and Hattie (age three). Drink says, "I got a bootleg life—my history is so messed up it's crossed up—like my music, and that's a bootleg answer."

Although Oma is identified in the census as being a farmer and Emma is not associated with a trade or profession, the family worked on the Davis farm as sharecroppers and performed other domestic and skilled labor, according to Drink. The system of sharecropping was instituted as a way to maintain and control the labor force required to sustain the thriving agricultural industry, particularly raising cotton. Many freedmen found themselves performing the same hard and monotonous work often on the same land where their families had lived and labored when they were slaves. At the end of each day, Oma or one of the older boys drove the wagon containing over one thousand pounds of cotton to the barn to be weighed by the overseer. Oma used his carpentry skills to fix up the outbuildings and structures on the Davis farm and was a pulp tree man (tree cutter). Emma most likely performed varied jobs such as picking cotton, washing clothes, cooking and butchering livestock. The older children would have worked with their parents picking cotton, while the younger ones may have been given the responsibility of watching their youngest siblings. However, children as young as four swept yards, carried water to field hands, fed work animals and drove cows out to pasture.

Life as a sharecropper for Oma and thousands of other freedmen and their descendants was one of hardship and poverty. Although the sharecropper and his or her family might have picked an excellent crop of cotton, when it was time to collect their share, the overseer would deduct money loaned to the family during the season for medication, clothing, food or other necessities. The majority of the time, sharecroppers would end up with little or nothing to show for their work. Then the debt was rolled over to the next season, and the cycle continued year after year. Families worked when they were sick and chose to go without food or clothing in an attempt to get ahead. Drink recalls that "on the Stuckey farm, the sharecroppers were paid $10 to $15 a month, depending on how much work your family did. We had about four different overseers—that I remember." On a farm with approximately fifty sharecroppers, however, the overseer might get paid $1,000 for the cotton season. Carrie Gass, one of Drink's childhood friends, describes the system this way: "Sharecropping is when we did their share of the work, and they got our share of the money."

In addition to sharecropping, carpentry and tree cutting, Drink said Oma was a "part-time preacher," a minister without a church. As a tree man engaged in the dangerous work of getting lumber out of the swamp areas and forest, Oma cut pulpwood into four- or five-foot-long pieces that were hauled on small trucks to the railroad yards, where the wood was loaded onto rail cars and hauled to the paper mills. Work was so plentiful during the late 1800s that Sumter County became the lumber capital of South Carolina, with thirty-one sawmills operating in 1884. Oma took his Bible with him into the swamp forests and did a little preaching from the back of a wagon. His deep voice cut through the air whenever the exhausted tree cutters stopped to rest. Oma's sermons gave the men just enough strength to make it through the day with prayerful pleas that Drink continues to shout: "Help me, Holy Ghost."

One day, tragedy struck the Small family. While Oma was sawing lumber, a pulpwood tree fell on him, killing him instantly. Accidents due to the dangerous work or worn-out equipment were not uncommon. Oma's death was difficult emotionally for his wife, Emma, and their children, including Drink's mother, Missy, who was just a young girl at the time. But loved ones grieved their loss on Sunday and went back to work on Monday. Oma's funeral was held on the Davis farm, and he was buried in the crowded cemetery that had been on the land since the antebellum period.

After Oma's death, Emma struggled to care for her large family. She did not have the resources to make necessary repairs to their house. The roof leaked, and they could see daylight through the gaping holes in the walls. The family used a cooking pot to collect the rainwater that dripped in through the ceiling. The house was too hot in summer and too cold in winter. To keep warm, family members huddled together as they slept, girls in one room, boys in the other. The fireplace provided heat but could not be left unattended. Emma increasingly relied on the labor of her four sons and four daughters to pay their debts. Everyone had to work harder and longer after Oma's death for the large family's survival. Unfortunately, due to circumstances beyond her control, not all of Emma's children survived. Sharecroppers and their families were highly susceptible to illness due to substandard, unsanitary living conditions and inadequate food and clothing.

Illness adversely impacted the Small family when the great influenza epidemic ravaged South Carolina from 1918 to 1919. Officials in Columbia, the state capital, encouraged residents to wear gauze masks, believing that this would prevent the spread of influenza. Physicians also promoted the use of Vick's VapoRub as a cure, but nothing helped. State officials responded by assigning a "colored Red Cross" to deliver food specifically prepared for African American patients. The rural communities were so isolated that it was extremely difficult to provide the care they needed. If neighbors did not help one another, families who were quarantined found themselves in a dire situation.

Drink's mother, Missy, was about thirteen when the influenza outbreak hit Lee County. "My momma's sister, the one everyone called Noon, had taken bad sick. Friends would bring food to the house, but they couldn't come in. The house had a door in the front, a door in the back and a 'cat crack' where friends would shove a little extra food through for the sick," Drink explains. Noon died as a result of the epidemic.

Shortly after her death, the house caught fire and burned to the ground. Everything was lost, including the family Bible that contained all the Small family's most important personal information, such as the full given names of the children and the dates of births and deaths. Emma and her seven children moved into a vacant house on the Davis property with only the clothes they had on their backs.

Throughout her life, Missy shared few stories about her childhood with her son. Drink recalls, "My momma was born in 1905 or '06 on the Davis farm, and that's where I was born. I guess we should have known more than we do about where we come from, but we don't…Just work, go to church, read the Bible if you knew how to read and work some more." Girls cleaned, cooked, sewed and searched for ways to keep younger siblings occupied and out of the way when there were jobs to be done. They also made homemade toys, such as apple core dolls, and played games with sticks and rocks. Most importantly, from the time a girl was old enough to be out on the farm alone, she learned how to be on alert for sexual advances from the overseer or hired help. Missy and her sisters knew not to be caught alone or in a situation where they were unable to run and hide.

Drink Small was born on January 28, 1933, the first and only child of Alice Small. His biological father, Arthur Jackson, and his mother never married, and he is not sure how or where his parents met. Although Arthur was from Bishopville, he rarely had contact with his son. Occasionally, Drink saw his father around town while he was attending high school. Arthur had at least four other children with various women. In spite of his father's lack of involvement, Drink was a happy child and found his early childhood years very special, albeit difficult. He explains, "I love this place—what I love best about Bishopville? Well, it produced me!"

Throughout his adult life, there have been questions and confusion about Drink's name. A 1986 music critic stated in the *Charleston Post and Courier* that "Drink" was a stage name he had taken fifty years earlier, and his given name was Richard. Drink balks, "It's D-R-I-N-K like a drink of liquor…Whoever said my name was Richard was wrong. There's no one named Richard in my family, and there is nothing rich about me. Better to say my name is Poor Drink, and I don't mean P-O-U-R." Additionally, in 2009, a music historian who published a document about noted blues and gospel musicians stated Drink's name as Frank "Drink" Small. Drink said, "People who see the name 'Drink' think that must be wrong. Nobody named Drink—must be uh, well, 'Frank,' so they change it in the paper." His unusual name did not seem to be a concern for his family, friends or the community where he grew up, however. He was simply known as "Drink." Missy named her only child Drink because she simply liked the way the first and last name sounded together: "Drink Small."

From the time Drink was born until he was in the ninth grade, his close-knit family lived and worked together. But Drink hated picking cotton. He says, "I picked a little cotton when I was a boy, but I weren't no good at it. You gotta know how to pick cotton, 'cause picking cotton will wear you out…God made me a guitar player, [and] that's why I gotta pick the hell out of that." Drink's mother frequently gave in to his persistent appeals to avoid cotton picking and allowed him to ride in the wagon with his Uncle Louis, who had taken a special interest in his nephew. During those rides, Louis would make sure the long hours were filled with music. Drink had been fascinated with music for as long as the family could remember. As the gray mule slowly pulled the wagon, Louis would sing or play his harmonica along the way, and Drink would often amuse his uncle and even try to engage his friends as they picked cotton with their family members. Drink explains, "I was always cutting up, trying to make everyone laugh." But not everyone felt like laughing when they were sweating in the cotton field, especially his friend Annie Lou Moses-Lane.

Annie Lou was born in 1922 on the Stuckey farm and fondly remembers growing up with Drink. She says, "Oh, I been knowing him all his life, since he was jus a little baby. I watch him at church for Missy sometime when she be singing in the choir. He was jus a baby used to be in church, suckin' on his momma's… [points to her breast and chuckles]." Annie Lou was baptized in the church in 1938. Annie Lou continued to be protective of Drink after his accident and tried to keep a watchful eye out for him whenever she could. She was like part of the Small family.

There were other family members living within walking distance of the Stuckey farm who would come to visit Drink and his family. As the only child in the household, he would sit on the floor near his mother sucking his thumb and carefully listening to everything the adults had to say. "See this thumb [he holds up his right thumb], it's crooked, ain't it? That's because [he points this thumb at an angle toward his mouth] I use to suck it all the time [laughs] like this," Drink explains. The Small family would share a simple meal while they laughed and swapped tales about strange and unusual occurrences. Stories about how to use roots to cure and ward off evil have always found a place in blues lyrics, as in "Red Mountain Blues" by H. Troy:

*Got myself some snakeroot, John the Conqueror, too*
*Chewed them both together, I know what they will do*
*Took some in my pocket, put some in my boot*
*That don't make him love me, I'll start right in to shoot.*

The stories were sometimes a way to pass the time or purely for entertainment. Drink said, "Lots of superstitious people in the country, your clothes hanging out a certain way, black cat cross your path. I got a good buddy; he's got some real crazy stories. He told me his cousin hunt coon, but he's blind, that the doctor even said his blind cousin hunt coon. Now how ya going to hunt coon if ya can't see? I told my buddy him and the doctor both lying! And he talk about wild hogs, wild hogs are dangerous, but my good buddy say his uncle raised wild hogs! I just make him talk, it's crazy. I said, 'How can you raise wild hogs?!' My buddy not just from the country, he from under the country!" Drink grew up with colorful stories and continued to use references to them, including the magical power of root working, in his music.

*"Charleston Women Blues"—Drink Small*

*I wrote a blues I call it the Charleston Women Blues. Charleston Women Blues.*
*Lord have mercy. Charleston Women Blues.*
*Can you hear the blues? Ha. Ha.*
*The Charleston women must be got roots on me.*
*The Charleston women must be got roots on me.*
*Every time I get ready to back to Columbia, South Carolina*
*Something about Charleston women, jus' won't let me leave.*
*One more time.*
*Charleston women, must be got roots on me, yeah-owah*
*Charleston women, I believe they got roots on me.*
*Every time I get ready to go back to Columbia, South Carolina*
*I don't want to leave.*
*I'm a single man. I don't have a wife.*
*I'm going to find me a girl in Charleston, one who can treat me nice.*
*You know them Charleston women, sure enough got roots on me.*
*When I finish playing in the club at night—*
*The Blues Doctor don't want to leave.*
*I live in Columbia, South Carolina, I don't live that far.*
*I can stick around tonight after we finish. I can take you down the street to a bar.*

*Cuz the Charleston women, I believe you got roots on me.*
*Because every time I try to go back to Columbia, South Carolina—*
*Something about the women, don't want me to leave.*
*I want to say something to all of y'all*
*I hope the women in Charleston have mercy on poor Drink Small.*
*Because Charleston women, I believe they got sure got a rot on me.*
*So look out fellows, cuz when I try to go back to Columbia, South Carolina—*
*But I think about them Charleston women—*
*I don't want to leave.*

The Small family also enjoyed listening to all types of music, including the risqué blues that were popular at the time. Songs like "I Want a Piece of a Your Pie" (Blind Lemon Johnson, 1938) and "Press My Button—Ring My Bell" (Lil Johnson, 1935) made a lasting impression on Drink, and he certainly wrote a number of "dirty blues" tunes of his own.

> *Way back about 1941, I don't know…'39 or '40…way back, like I said I was a kid. They* [relatives] *come around singing, that's why I can remember rhyming things. They had a song they used to sing when I was a boy. My grandmomma say, "Way it is, Uncle Bill?" He was a tall man, he could, a-ah read the cards a little bit. Excuse my language now! "Way it is?" and he sings, excuse my language* [he recites]. *"Push it up. Shove it up. I don't want to spend the night, with my hand just on that thang—Putang!"* [laughs] *My grandmomma say, "Ooh, Uncle Bill, I clare—I don't know what I'm gonna do with you!" I was a little boy playing 'round; they never knew I heard all that!*

Many years later, while entertaining students at the University of South Carolina, Drink was always asked to sing an all-time favorite: his version of the 1935 raunchy blues song by Lil Johnson, "Get 'Em from the Peanut Man (Hot Nuts)."

*"Get 'Em from the Peanut Man (Hot Nuts)"—Lil Johnson*

*Sellin' nuts, hot nuts, anybody here want to buy my nuts?*
*Sellin' nuts, hot nuts, I've got nuts for sale*
*One for five, two for ten,*
*If you buy 'em once, you'll buy 'em again*
*Sellin' nuts, hot nuts, you buy 'em from the peanut man…*
*(spoken: Hot nuts? Peanuts! Nutsies? Nuts!)*

*Sellin' nuts, hot nuts, anybody here want to buy some nuts?*
*Sellin' nuts, hot nuts, I've got nuts for sale*
*You see that man all dressed in brown,*
*He's got the hottest nuts in town*
*Sellin' nuts, hot nuts, you buy 'em from the peanut man*
*Nuts, hot nuts, anybody here want to buy my nuts?*
*Sellin' nuts, hot nuts, I've got nuts for sale*
*When a hog gets hungry, he begins to grunt,*
*When a man gets hungry, he begins to hunt,*
*For nuts, hot nuts, you buy 'em from the peanut man*

Everyone in the family participated in music, according to Drink. "My momma, she could sing. Uncle Joe played the guitar and Fender organ. Louis played the harmonica—mouth harp. My Aunt Carrie had a singing group, the Harlem Singers," he explains. Missy knew her son was more focused on music than she or her brothers and sisters had ever been. Drink's family and friends realized he was a musical prodigy at a young age. He soon began playing the piano and pump organ, and he made several guitars, including one with rubber bands and a broomstick and another cut from a tire's inner tube. Drink began creating his own songs and enjoying childhood rhymes, especially about animals. Rhymes he recalled included, "Jacob had a donkey, swapped him for a monkey…" After the wagon accident, he was assigned light chores, and these tasks became the subject of his melodies. He recalls, "I took care of the animals, mules, chickens, the cow. I always had dogs; must have had thirteen

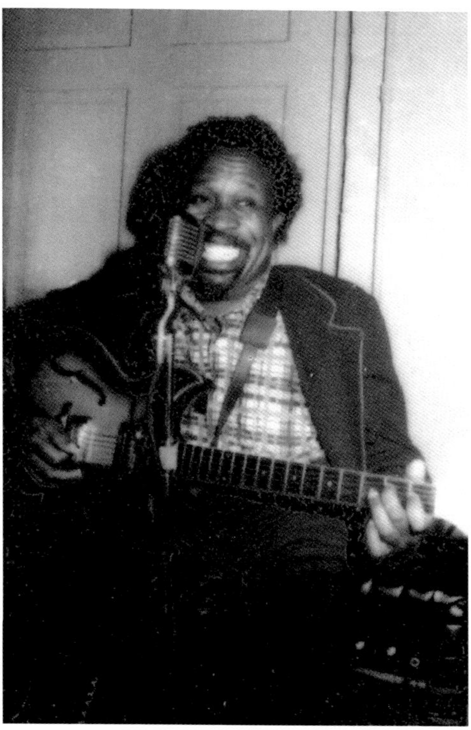

A 1979 photo of Drink playing at Group Therapy club, Five Points, Columbia, South Carolina. *Courtesy of Drink Small, personal collection.*

dogs. You have to take care of your dog too, don't you? If you don't, who gonna do it? You make corn bread for the family, and I made dog bread too."

Coon dogs, farm chores and barnyard animals continued to find their way into his lyrics as an adult. "I think they have 'bout six different kind of coon dogs, and I got a song about that [laughs]." The coon dog continued to hold a special place in Drink's heart throughout his life, and his own pet coon dogs have been featured in newspaper and magazine photographs and even paintings.

Many times when Missy would take over her son's cow milking chore, Drink would find a place behind the barn to play his little homemade guitar while the chickens strutted and pecked in the dirt around him. One of Drink's humorous original animal songs is titled "Too Much Water to Be Funky."

*There's too much water, too much water to be funky*
*Go and get yourself a bar of soap—*
*And stop going around smelling like a donkey...*

Drink was happiest when he was with his mother, entertaining her and making her laugh. Missy loved being with her son, especially when they were together at church. The Smalls were a deeply religious family. During the week, Drink attended school and did farm chores, but on Sunday, he went to church like everyone else on the Stuckey farm. Attending the Jerusalem Stuckey Baptist Church was a spirit-filled experience. It was not uncommon for someone to get carried away by the message and begin shouting, dancing or even occasionally speaking in tongues. There was always a church mother dressed in a white nurse's uniform standing in the aisle ready to assist anyone who became overcome with the spirit. Annie Lou remembers, "We didn't have anything [sophisticated instrumentation], didn't have to play a piano, as long as we could [she demonstrated] wave and clap our hands."

A strong bond with the church was something Drink always shared with his mother. Drink often walked with his mother and grandmother to neighboring churches where they worshiped and fellowshipped with family and friends. He says, "All these other people were still our neighbors; country neighbors might be six or seven plantation farms away." The family also attended camp meeting revivals. Drink usually wore a suit jacket (to conceal his disfigured shoulder), short pants and a shirt with a bow tie. On special occasions, Missy would part his hair to one side, pressing it flat against his head with a thick layer of lard pomade. No matter how hot the

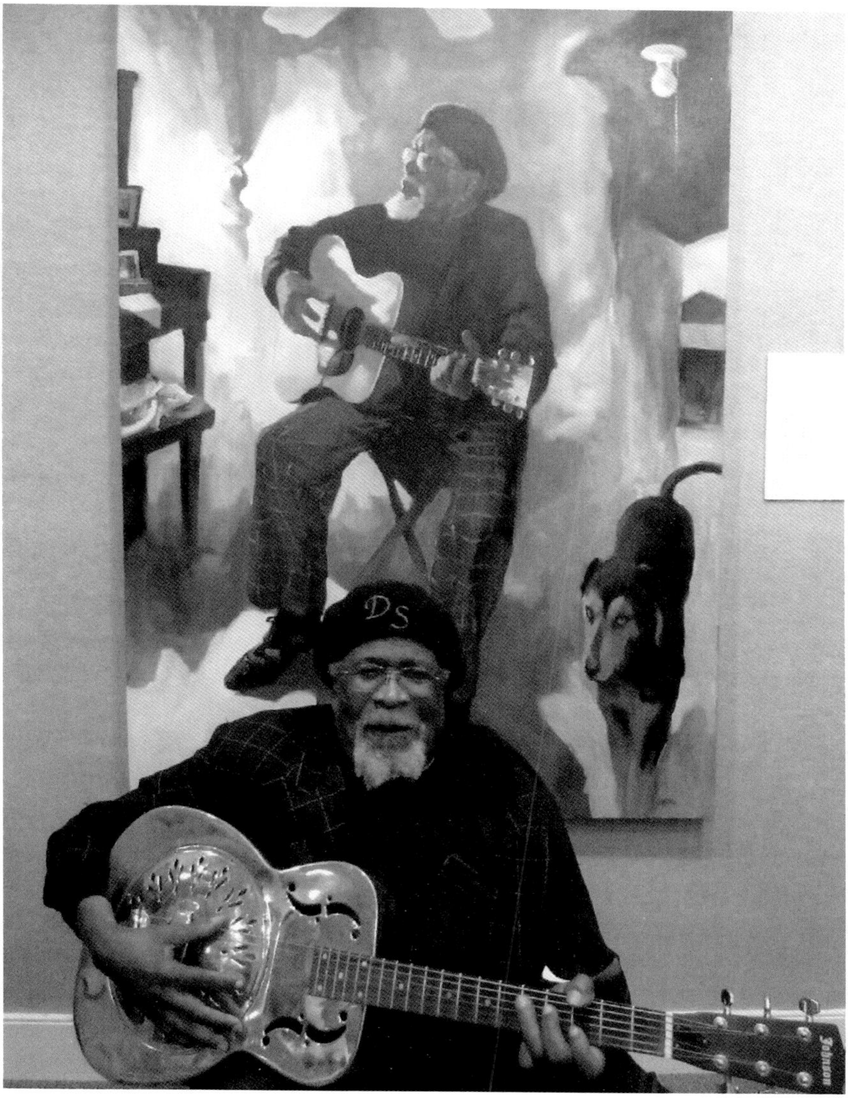

Drink sits in front of a portrait by Glenn Miller at the Burroughs and Chapin Museum, Myrtle Beach, South Carolina. Photograph taken and copyrighted 2011. *Courtesy of Clair DeLune, from the personal collection of Drink Small.*

weather or how long the church service lasted, Drink would sit under a tree listening to ministers preaching and choirs singing traditional spirituals and gospel music.

Drink was a polite and extremely well-mannered little boy. Children were required to be respectful. Drink was expected to learn to read and write. Drink was an excellent student and noted, "I ain't got a lot of education, but I got a lot of dedication." Two women taught grades one through seven in the little two-room schoolhouse next to the church. Drink remembers his teachers well. He says, "Ms. Easter Reynolds had gone to college; the other lady had only gone up to the eleventh grade." Children who wanted to attend school beyond the seventh grade enrolled in the school in town of Bishopville. "The teachers [in my primary school] were not [approved] to teach material beyond a seventh grade level, but they took it on themselves to teach eighth grade subjects to those children that stayed on," explains Drink. Many of his classmates stopped attending school after the fifth or sixth grade, as their parents needed them to help pick cotton. It was very unusual for a child, especially a boy, to remain in school. Drink says, "I was pretty smart, and the teachers liked me, so I stayed on. There wasn't but three of us there by then; I was the only boy in the eighth grade [at the Stuckey school]."

As a child, Drink could not imagine living anyplace else. He had his family, his school, his church—what more could a little boy want? The Stuckey farm might have been more than enough for a little boy; however, for many adult black men, the injustice and humiliation they often experienced working day in and day out as sharecroppers had few redeeming qualities. In 1941, Joseph Small left the Stuckey farm to fight in World War II. He was gone for four years. Joe wanted to get away and left his old guitar for his nephew to play. Louis remained on the farm. He felt responsible for the accident in the cotton field and never forgave himself for the terrible incident that resulted in his nephew's physical deformity and recurring pain. Louis worked hard and constantly apologized to Missy for the accident and begged his nephew to forgive him. Missy never blamed her brother for the accident, but Drink's pain was a constant reminder.

Drink began spending time with an older sharecropper on the farm who was a popular, talented guitar player. Annie Lou explains, "Greenback, he the one that taught Drink to play [the guitar]." Greenback lived in the smokehouse, a small outbuilding with one door and no windows. The building was used to preserve meat and fish. The years Drink spent with Greenback were the closest thing he ever had to a formal music education for guitar. Drink says:

> *Greenback, he was the best guitar player in Lee County…had a new guitar he got from Walter Fields or one of them—uh—them, yeah,*

> *them mail-order companies. I got a song I wrote about him, I don't remember how go—you gotta look it up* [singing]*: "There was guitar player, down in Bishopville, he was a man and I was a boy—dah, dah, dee dah, dah. He was a guitar player, never been married in his life. Everyone called him Greenback and his real name was Roy Price. Yeah, he was a guitar player…"*

By the time Joe returned from the war, Drink was playing the guitar as well as Greenback. Emma was thrilled to have Joe home again, and the family needed his help. Joe joined his brothers and plowed for a short time; however, after the war, he was never comfortable being on the farm again. The family knew it was only a matter of time before Joe would leave the farm for good. It was Emma and her failing health that kept him working on the farm as long as he did. Emma was in her late seventies. She had lived a very hard life working long hours, exposed to the elements and suffering countless physical and emotional challenges.

Drink was fourteen when his grandmother Emma died. Emma was buried next to her husband, Oma, and her daughter, the girl everyone called Noon (Hattie). After the matriarch passed away, Pickett took his younger brother Oma Jr., and they moved to Columbia, South Carolina. Eventually, Joe headed up north to New Jersey, and Louis remained dutifully on the farm. Soon Drink's aunts Carrie and Sarah both married and moved to neighboring farms. Between World War II and the great migration north, some sharecroppers paid off their debts and others just walked away. Life on the Stuckey farm was changing. Roland Smith, one of Drink's childhood friends who was also in the cotton field at the time of his accident, says that after Joe left the farm, Drink spent all his time with Greenback, playing the guitar. Roland left the farm to go and fight in the war. Drink resented the war, explaining, "We had German prisoners working in the cotton field; they were prisoners and was treated better and paid more than us who grew up and worked there all our lives.

The South Carolina Historical Society confirms Drink's memories of the good treatment the German POWs received in his home state. In September 1943, when 250 German POWs were brought to a temporary camp in Bamberg County, the county agricultural extension agent wrote, "There was almost a steady flow of traffic by the camp. People from miles around came to see what was taking place. [Even after they were banned from the camp area]…they never lost interest in the camp and its prisoners of war." Within a few weeks, the Bamberg County agent reported that POWs were even "entertained" in local residents' homes. Despite the fact that these were prisoners who had recently fought to kill American troops, if not the sons of the Bamberg families who employed them, this bond between Germans and Americans grew during their weeks of association. Drink recalls, "We'd sit out back at supper time eating corn bread off the back of the truck or on a tree stump, looking through the window of the Stuckey house and watching prisoners being served dinner at the table."

*I remember those days, walking behind the plow.*
*I look at my poor mama, mama milking the cow.*
*The houses where I used to live, they done tore 'em all down.*
*That's in Bishopville, my hometown.*

Life on the Stuckey farm was not the same for the family after Emma passed. Alice Small was accustomed to being surrounded by her close-knit family, but so many things had changed. Thankfully, the Jerusalem Stuckey Baptist Church continued to provide Missy and her son with a sense of family, community and purpose. Annie Lou and Deacon Moses were still there, along with a few others. Missy and Drink continued to attend camp meeting revivals at other churches as they had always done with Emma. These day trips broke up the monotony of the day-to-day work and gave visiting families something special to look forward to. While visiting a church in Rembert, South Carolina, Drink met an extraordinary musician by the name of Albert Smith who could play the piano better than anyone inside or out of the church. "He played those songs the people been singing all their lives. I went down when they funeralized him—I think he was about ninety—and I was sad when he passed on," Drink recalls. Drink would accompany Albert on the guitar, and sometimes Albert would sing and Drink would play the piano. It was an eye-opening experience, Drink explains: "He was a man and I was a boy, but I could still keep up. That's how good I had gotten."

Drink continued to listen to his favorite stations broadcasting from Nashville to Charlotte: WLAC, WCKY, WIS and WBT. He loved the music of Fats Domino, John Lee Hooker, Muddy Waters, Lightnin' Slim and Lightnin' Hopkins. Drink learned to play boogie-woogie, gospel, country and bluegrass, though his mother didn't always approve. "My momma called it the 'devil's music' and did not want her son playing with them 'trifling and no good men.' She didn't really want me playing anything that was not gospel music or going any place but church or school," he said.

After completing eighth grade at the Jerusalem Stuckey primary school in 1949, it was time for Drink to move on to high school. There were limited options available for African Americans in South Carolina's segregated education system. "Where you went to school was depending on a family's circumstances," Drink recalls. "If your family had some money, you could go to Camden, [where] there was the Mather Academy." Mather Academy, founded in 1887 by the Women's Home Missionary Society of the Methodist Episcopal Church, was established to educate the children of former slaves and their descendants. The school was originally named the Browning Model Home and Industrial School and built on a twenty-seven-acre former plantation site. Mather's prestigious reputation and rigorous academic curriculum centered on Christian values. In 1959, the school merged with the Boylan Haven School of Jacksonville, Florida, to become Boylan Haven–Mather Academy. It closed in 1983, and the building was demolished by 1995. Drink stated, "James Clyburn [U.S. representative, D-SC], his momma went there. Leon Howard's [South Carolina state representative] auntie did, too. I knew them, but I didn't go to the Mather school." Missy did not have the financial resources to send her son to the private school; however, she did not want him to stay home either. Missy wanted her son to have an education.

Some African American children attended informal classes in the homes of their neighbors who had learned to read and write. In the Browntown community near the Scape Ore Swamp more recently associated with the infamous Lizard man lore, Al Wilson used to teach children and adults out of his house.

The high school Drink attended became a significant place for his early musical career. In 1936, two new segregated schools had been constructed in Bishopville. Noted architect Henry Dudley Harrall designed Bishopville High School for the white students at a cost of about $71,000. Edgeworth and McBride Contractors of Cheraw constructed Dennis High School for Bishopville's black students at a cost of $17,500 on land donated by local philanthropist Rebecca Dennis.

The white students not only had a new school built, but they also received a school bus to go with it. "We didn't have a school bus. A white lady donated a big ol' nine-passenger station wagon for the black children who was rural. We had twenty-two people riding, counting Mr. Bob Crosby, the driver. Girls had to sit on the boys' laps to make room, so I had no problem with that!" Drink recalls. Some of his classmates walked to school, including Carrie Gass, who lived in town and trekked two and a half miles on foot to and from Dennis High. The school offered grades one through eleven. All the textbooks were secondhand or discarded by Bishopville High School. Instead of Drink being the only boy in a class of three students, he was now in a school where fifty or sixty children attended from all over the county. He was popular and funny. Carrie says, "Drink could win people over with his personality, and he could really play the guitar. We never heard anyone in Bishopville play like that!"

Drink loved high school and continued to write and sing songs. He wrote "Bishopville Women," inspired by the attractive young women at Dennis High, and recoreded it more than forty years later:

> [spelling] *B-i-s-h-o-p. V-i-l-l-e*
> *Spell Bishopville baby, that is home for me.*
> *That is home for me.*
> *Uh umm, mmm, mmm.*
> *Uh mmm, mmm mmm. Ah-hmm, Ah-hum, ah hum.*
> *Ain't no other women, be any finer.*
> *All the pretty women down there prettiest in South Carolina.*
> *Them Bishopville women, them Bishopville women, they sure look fine to me.*
> *Uh umm, mmm, mmm.*
> *Uh mmm, mmm mmm. Ah-hmm, Ah-hum, ah humm*
> *Down in Bishopville, where I finished high school,*
> *All the girls love me down there, always call me cool.*
> *Those Bishopville women, those Bishopville women*
> *They sure, look fine, to me.*
> [humming] *Uh umm, mmm, mmm. Uh mmm, mmm mmm. Ah-hmm,*
> *Ah-hum, ah hum.*

Shortly after Drink enrolled in Dennis High School, he met Mrs. J. Leobraska Sally, a creative new music teacher from North Carolina. She developed a strong culture and the arts curriculum that also included a very popular glee club. Under her tutelage, Drink received vocal coaching. He was the only male in the school who could sing the deep bass harmony part. He performed with the glee club and played piano for the group. During his first year in high school, Drink also formed a group, the Six Stars. Carrie explains, "I mean, Drink could really play and could sing, too. All Ned [Hickman] and Lucius [Sylvester] had to do was stand behind Drink." The group's most popular song was "Mule Train." Frankie Laine recorded the humorous western-style cowboy song in 1949, and it reached number one on

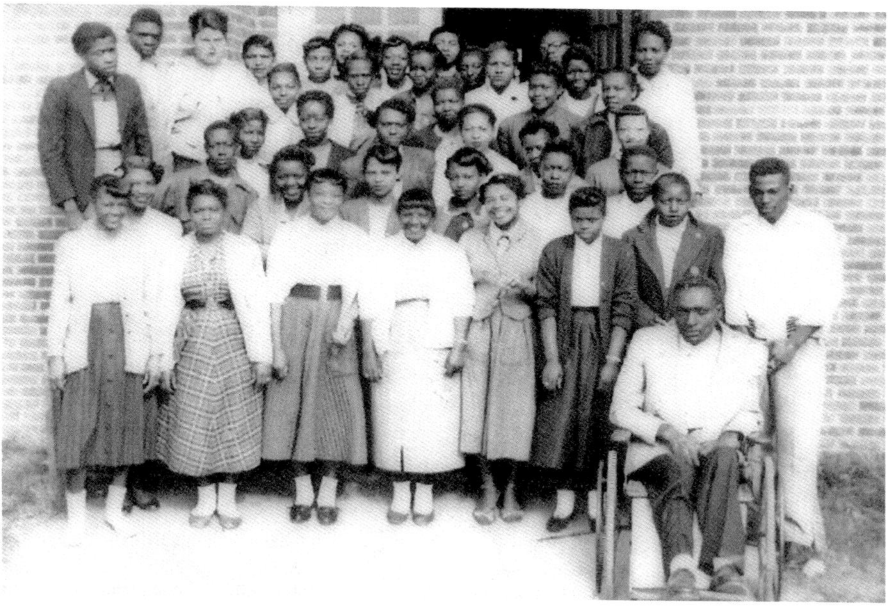

The 1953 Dennis High School senior class picture. Drink Small is in the top row, left, wearing a dark jacket. *Courtesy of Drink Small.*

the *Billboard* magazine chart in November of that year. Drink imitated Laine's recording, including a narration with a perfect cowboy ranch voice, whistle and whip-cracking effect by slapping the back of his guitar. The majority of the time, Drink and his friends did not get paid for their performances. The other boys were not serious, however; they were just out having a good time. Drink was totally focused on music. The Six Stars disbanded. He formed the Golden Five, and the group performed together until he left Bishopville.

*Chapter 2*

# DRINK SMALL DOES IT ALL

Like many of his high school friends, Drink liked traveling to neighboring towns to see movies and other live performances, which enabled him to view another one of his musical heroes in film. Drink explains, "They had a theater in Camden called the Haigler Theater. That's a place, used to be a theater there where the blacks used to go from Bishopville over there. I saw Louis Jordan—they did three different movies on Louis Jordan. One of 'em was *Two Gun Jordan*, one of 'em was *Beware* [1946] and one was *Run Joe* [1948]. I was in high school. The Haigler Theater, they used to bring up the big shows." The theater had approximately 542 seats and was located at the intersection of Broad and Rutledge Streets. It was named in honor of the Catawba chief King Haigler, who had befriended early area European settlers. Between the radio and the theater, Drink's list of musical influences continued to expand. He recalls, "I liked it all: Amos Melburn, Duke Ellington, them other fellas, Lionel Hampton and Tommy Dorsey. I listened to 'em all."

On Friday night, crowds of men and women, eager to forget the backbreaking work done throughout the week, piled into the makeshift clubs in the county, often tucked away down dusty roads. These jook joints (or juke joints) offered live music and the opportunity to dance, drink, flirt and fight. Local musicians like Greenback had a steady following at places like the Davis Country Club, a large two-story nightspot on the back side of thirty acres of wooded land. According to a Davis family descendant, the biracial descendants of James Ellis Stuckey and Nellie Slater Stuckey owned the property. Family oral history notes that one of James and Nellie's daughters, Nina Vermelle Stuckey, fell in love with and married an African American laborer by the name of Munson Davis. After they married and Nellie inherited the land, they built the gathering place for their extended family and other African American friends and neighbors. Greenback performed there, and he was happy to have Drink play the guitar for a few minutes while he went around back and drank whiskey. Everyone wanted to hear the popular songs performed like the original artists. If a musician could sing "Messin' Around" like Memphis Slim or "Long About Midnight" like Roy Brown, the crowd kept dancing.

Drink had long since learned to master and embellish all the rhythm and soul hits, and his reputation for providing flawless impersonations of the best songs from the Harlem Hit Parade got around. He was so popular with the local club owners that they soon became more interested in hiring him for their clubs than Greenback. The older guitar player collected half his pay in whiskey, and as the night wore on, Greenback would get so intoxicated he could barely sit up, let alone play the guitar. At that time, Drink was not at the club for the liquor or girls, he didn't fight and he could play all night and never run out songs. Drink explains, "Greenback was being paid $1.50 a night and all the whiskey he wanted. I had my own deal: $3.00 a night and you keep your liquor. This was a lot of money, more money than a man could make in a week plowing a field."

As a young musician, Drink could be heard playing the guitar all over Lee County. His trio was playing for high school dances, and he was traveling throughout the state with the glee club. On Sunday mornings, Drink always played gospel music at the Jerusalem Stuckey Baptist Church or another church in the area. On Friday and Saturday nights, he would play his guitar in the rowdy juke joints and clubs. Because of his musical skill, Drink was often called upon to fill in for some out-of-town singer who needed local musicians for a large gospel extravaganza or concert. He recalls, "I was boogalooin' on Saturday night and hallalujehin' in church on Sunday." As happy as he was, he could not escape personal loss. "In '49, Greenback got burned up in a fire on the white people's farm, got burned up in the little house he was living in, the smokehouse. Lord, I can't recall how that song go. You gonna have to look it up," he sighs.

*I know a guitar player, live in my hometown Bishopville*
*Every time I heard him play guitar, gave my little heart a thrill*
*He was a guitar player, never been married in his life.*

*He was known the name of Greenback, but his real name was Roy Price.*
*He got burnt up on a Sunday night, round '47 or '49*
*Lot of time to think of Greenback, that day run through my mind*
*He was a guitar player, never been married in his life.*
*He was known the name of Greenback, but his real name was Roy Price.*
*He drank a lot of moonshine, he liked to drink a lot.*
*But he played his guitar, and he could make a beat-up guitar have feel*
*He was a guitar player, never been married in his life.*
*He was known the name of Greenback, but his real name was Roy Price*
*It hurt me that next Monday morning after Greenback got burnt up*
*It hurt me to my heart, that, oh, that was just so tough enough*
*He was a guitar player, never been married in his life.*
*He was known the name of Greenback, but his real name was Roy Price.*
*I wanna let the people know, want everybody know the name*
*Lot of people know him Greenback, the real name they never did know.*
*He was a guitar player, Lord know never been married in his life*
*He was known the name of Greenback, but his real name was Roy Price.*
*He was known the name of Greenback, but his real name was Roy Price.*

After Drink graduated from high school, he enrolled in the Denmark Trade School in Bamberg County, a two-hour bus ride from Bishopville. Drink arrived on the campus on a Tuesday night and was greeted by Luns C. Richardson (current president of Morris College), who was then the dean of men. Drink says, "Cleveland Sellers [currently Voorhees College president and noted South Carolina civil rights activist] and three other preachers owned some little army barracks that had bunk beds in it. Dean put me in room 14; some teachers were in room 13. Soon as I got in my room, I started playing guitar. Five more boys in the room, we were having fun." Drink recalled the campus had a canteen where the students socialized. The first Saturday night after he arrived, the school held a talent contest. "It was 1952, same year B.B. King had come out with his 'Three O'clock Blues.' I didn't have an electric guitar; I played the regular guitar. I made my own song. I could always play a boogie, so I played the 'Denmark Boogie,' and I turned it out! I won the talent contest, and I was known all over the campus." He was enrolled in the barbering program and rode the bus back home on the weekends or, more often, to his next paying gig. Due to his physical condition, Drink Small never learned to drive a car.

While attending Denmark and still performing with the Golden Five, Drink meet Kipling "Kip" Taquana Anderson from Starr, South Carolina, a small town in Anderson County. Kip was attending South Carolina State College, a historically black institution in Orangeburg, and had started playing the guitar for a female gospel group. The young men often played on the same programs together and became friends. Drink successfully completed the barber certificate program and worked for a short time at a barbershop in Sumter, South Carolina. Drink says, "I knew I wasn't going to cut hair; I wanted to cut up." He was creating a life for himself beyond the Stuckey farm.

After Drink left home, he sent a portion of his earnings to assist his uncles who were managing the family's debts. Drink explains, "We were poor, but we weren't the poorest people there. When Joe got back from the war, he and my other uncles made a deal with a man in Columbia, and they bought a 1929 A Model Ford." This gave the family the opportunity to choose other work if they desired. Drink's mother, Missy, was no longer physically capable of doing hard farm work, so she found a small house for them to live in. As an only child, Drink was concerned about his mother's health and said, "My momma, she was staying by herself most of the time on John McCutchin's place down the street from my [new] church. The white lady, Irene, she iron clothes for her, washed for her, lived next door to her. My momma had been hurt on the farm. She had arthritis, so this other lady—see, I got so much to say; it don't make sense, but it make sense to me. So see, about three or four miles down the road, they had a straw factory. Down there they called it rheumatism, okay rheumatism—worked on the farm, so this other lady say, 'Let's go down and break broom straw.' You know broom straw? Down in the country they make yard brooms. It [the factory] about three or four miles. This man that make medicine told my momma, 'Don't you walk down there Missy!'...but the other lady persuaded her. After that, her rheumatism got real bad, [and] she had to go to the hospital. She walked with a limp ever since," he recalls. Drink ran errands, went grocery shopping and helped Missy in any way he could. However, he was conflicted. He was meeting some of the finest gospel musicians in the country. Should he continue to take care of his mother or should he pursue a career in music? Drink had made a commitment when he was in high school: he promised Missy that somehow he would find a way to do both.

Drink was committed to honoring his promise to provide for his mother. When he would meet someone from one of the professional quartets while in Columbia, Greenville, Spartanburg or Charleston, he would make sure that they knew he was for hire. Drink would also reach out to the rural church pastors and encourage them to host small gospel concerts for the professional groups passing through the state. This was a way for the visiting bands to make a little extra money and have a nice home-cooked meal. Drink would always have his group be the opening act. According to Drink, "The little gospel group I was with, we were bringing all the major groups [national gospel recording artist] down there [to Sumter, Clarendon and Lee Counties]: the Swanee Quintet, the Nightingales, the Chosen Gospel Choir, Sister Rosetta Tharpe. A couple of times they come by my hometown to try and find me. They see the name Bishopville, they think I'm in Bishopville, they didn't know it another fifteen mile out to the country." The Golden Five played everywhere, from local country and storefront churches to the largest churches in the state. Some Sundays they would do more than one program, and they traveled to Columbia frequently. Whenever one of the featured musical groups needed a guitar player to fill in, they all wanted Drink. "I was half famous before I left there, 'cause every time there was a concert, I'd be the guitar player, and I sing bass, I had a bad bass voice. I was like a monkey wrench. I got a long range of voice, singing in the quartet, singing the blues, the high part by myself, a cappella. My name had gotten out there, and we were playing for some big-time groups. Before I left Bishopville, I done been to Pittsburgh, Philadelphia, Baltimore," he recalls. Drink quickly realized he was more valuable to the professional groups as an independent guitar player.

African American musicians from South Carolina who found professional outlets for their talent inspired Drink to take a similar path. In 1946, Spartanburg super talent Julius "June" Cheeks joined the Nightingales and recorded for Decca Records. By 1953, June had made another important move to Sam Cooke's Soul Stirrers. Additionally, gospel groups such as the Dixie Hummingbirds, Pilgrim Travelers, Swan Silvertones, Sensational Nightingales and Five Blind Boys of Mississippi were attracting white audiences. Musicians Drink knew and even played with were achieving stardom. The stories of gospel music success like the Pilgrim Travelers receiving a new Cadillac every year and quartets making $700 or $800 for a single performance were all he needed to hear. If he could earn money like that playing music, he would have no problem providing for his mother. "I had to leave Bishopville. I couldn't make no money. If you can't make no money, what you gonna do? I had to leave, and I knew I was good enough," he explains. The gospel music industry had changed since he was on the Stuckey farm, and he wanted to be part of it.

Drink understood the subtle and intricate style differences of musicians he admired like Sister Rosetta Tharpe, a pioneer who could excite an audience with her unusual vocal pitch while accompanying herself on steel guitar. Drink would play her records and make his fingers copy each chord until he could blend it with other sounds to perfectly create his own unique style. Drink explains, "Greenback played it like this. Tennessee Ernie Ford like this. Sister Rosetta Tharpe used this chord and make it kind of bluesy. And you gotta give it some pressure like…over this here chord, oh yeah!" These were the golden years of gospel music.

In the late 1940s, three leading members of the gospel music community—Rebert Harris, Charlie Bridges and Abraham Battle—established a society dedicated to the advancement of quartet singing, training, education and supporting black gospel groups. The society also hosted the National Quartet Convention in California as an attempt to professionalize the industry and make it a more profitable venture. In South Carolina, Charles Derrick was committed to doing the very same thing. Derrick, as he was known, was born in Lexington, South Carolina, a small community with a large gospel footprint. Lexington's African American churches hosted praise conventions that showcased five or six choirs. Gospel artists from around the state participated, helping to establish the Greater Columbia area, along with Greenville in the Upstate region, as important cities for South Carolina's gospel music culture. Charles Derrick came from a family of means. His father was a barber and owned a dry cleaning store; his mother was a schoolteacher. Both of his parents led church choirs on the weekends, and Derrick learned about business and gospel music at a very early age.

Derrick began his radio career in Charlotte, North Carolina, and in 1953, he returned to Columbia to serve as the chief disc jockey for WOIC radio station. WOIC, founded in 1947, was owned by Speidel Broadcasters, Inc., which also controlled the licensees of WTMP, Tampa, Florida; WPAL, Charleston, South Carolina; WYNN, Florence, South Carolina; WSOK, Savannah, Georgia; and WHIH, Portsmouth, Virginia. The programming concept was to address the radio needs and preferences of the black community. The president, Joe Speidel III, was the majority stockholder, with local supervision administered by Speidel or other Speidel senior management staff. Management was white, while the majority of the program staff was black. For the Columbia station, Joe Speidel hired Charles Derrick, Paris Eley, Charles "Big Saul" Greene, Reverend William McKinley Bowman and others to create relevant programming and deliver the news. Derrick, a musician, booked and promoted groups such as the Clovers, and he wrote songs that earned royalties until his death. Ethel Taylor, who worked for WOIC as a host for over forty-four years, was named one of the top five female announcers in the United States by *Billboard* magazine in 1973. Her popular WOIC program, *A Date with Ethel*, provided an eclectic mix of music, announcements of community events, recipes and recordings of high school glee clubs.

Listeners who tuned in to WOIC between the hours of 10:00 a.m. and 12:00 p.m. could hear the popular gospel musical show *Wings of Faith*, hosted by Reverend Bowman. Reverend Bowman deejayed the early morning and afternoon gospel programs at the station for over two decades, served as pastor of Second Nazareth Baptist Church and owned a record label, Bowman Records. Derrick was inspired by the popularity of the gospel program and formed a male quartet, the Spiritualaires of Columbia, South Carolina.

Reverend Bowman provided the financing, and Derrick recorded the group at WOIC on the Bowman label in 1955. The Spiritualaires had many different talented members at various times. Opal Luis Nation, a British music historian and writer who was influential in bringing African American musicians to London in the 1960s, noted that the first Spiritualaires of Columbia, South Carolina, consisted of Charles Derrick on bass and drums; Jimmy Foster on lead vocals; Fred Davis as tenor; Sonny Boy as high tenor; Johnny (from Florida) on second lead guitar; and Sergeant Rose, a gentleman Derrick heard play at nearby Fort Jackson, on guitar.

However, Nation reports that the second time Charles Derrick recorded the group, the personnel had changed and now included Luis Johnson, Joseph Hollis, Charles Gavish, Bernard Caldwell, Norris Tuner, Johnny (from Florida) and a man named Mr. Kimpson on guitar. Charles Derrick sent one demo to Leonard Allen at United Records, and Allen recorded the group on October 14, 1954. However, he never released any of the recordings. By 1955, the original members of the Spiritualaires had gone their separate ways, prompting Derrick to be on the lookout for new musicians for the popular male quartet. He believed that black musicians in South Carolina could compete on the national gospel market and was always watching and listening for star quality. Derrick knew that Drink Small was one of the local musicians favored by many touring professionals. Bandleaders and concert organizers regularly hired Drink and asked for him by name. Derrick understood that one of those groups would certainly hire Drink full time if the opportunity ever presented itself. He was not going to pass up the opportunity.

Drink's course work at Denmark Trade School ended in September; however, he wanted to participate in the graduation ceremony in June 1955. After his graduation, Derrick invited Drink to become a member of his Columbia-based quartet. This was the opportunity Drink had been waiting for—his chance to work full time as a musician. Columbia was an ideal place to launch his musical career. Derrick was a well-respected and connected businessman, and Columbia was only a short bus ride away from Missy and Bishopville. Drink said, "I got my cousin 'Judge,' Aunt Carrie's son [Ernest Holloman]. We called him Judge because he had a real long head, looked like he ought to be a judge. I got him to come stay with my momma, then I slip off over here to Columbia."

*I was raised in the country in a little old shack.*
*I moved to Columbia, South Carolina, and I didn't went back.*
*Houses where I used to live they done tore them all down.*
*That is in Bishopville, that my hometown.*

In July 1955, a talented, happy, twenty-two-year-old Drink Small moved to Columbia, South Carolina, to join Charles Derrick and the WOIC family of musicians, fulfilling his lifelong dream. He mother had been right: God had spared his life, and great things were going to happen. He had worked harder than anyone he knew and never given up. Now his chance had arrived. It was an easy move for Drink to make because he lived with his uncle Oma Small Jr., who had rented a house on Stark Street, the site where Fellowship Baptist Church is located today. Since her son had a place to live, family and respectable "grown folk" to watch out for him, Drink's mother was happy that he could finally pursue his lifelong dream. She had always believed in him. He was special; he was Drink. Now he was a member of the Spiritualaires of Columbia, South Carolina.

WOIC was an exciting place to work, and Drink spent as much time as he could at the station. He said, "From North Main Street you turn right on Sunset, cross the tracks, take a little dirt road off Sunset. You could see the radio station from Sunset." Derrick's new radio dial-in request show, *Dial Derrick*, brought to WOIC top talent of the day, such as the Cadets, a doo-wop group from Los Angeles, and the Charms, who recorded a number-one rhythm and blues hit, "Hearts of Stone." Drink met and learned from musicians from all over the United States because he was now affiliated with Charles Derrick. The radio station was well used as a common meeting space for aspiring black musicians such as the Clovers, Sammy Cooke (not the same individual as Sam Cooke of the Soul Stirrers) and the Keynotes and Otis Goodman and the Pontiacs.

By the time Drink joined the Spiritualaires, the group included Louis Johnson, Joseph Hollis, Charles Derrick, Bernard Caldwell, Norris Turner and A.J. Thompson. Drink was a member of the group in February 1956 when Derrick negotiated with Vee-Jay for the Spiritualaires' recordings of "Can't Hide Sinner" and "When the Saints Go Marching In."

Vee-Jay Records—founded in 1953 in Gary, Indiana, by Vivian Carter and James C. Bracken, who used their first initials for the label's name—was then the most successful black-owned record company in the country. There was plenty of recording and performing work for a talented young musician. With his versatility, Drink worked nonstop.

Being on the Vee-Jay Record label in such a short period of time was more than Drink could have imagined. He was a long way from the cotton field; he was finally in the big league.

The early success of the Spiritualaires reinforced the decision Drink had made to leave Bishopville. The station's call letters said it all—WOIC: We Originate In Columbia. WOIC's enterprising disc jockeys like Reverend Bowman, Samson T. Spencer and Louis Summers eagerly promoted local and regional African American musicians, intellectuals and business leaders through their programming. Derrick, who was seven years older than Drink, proved to be more than a business manager. In those early years, Derrick served as a mentor, father figure and friend to his protégé. Drink recalls that he idolized the successful businessman. Derrick managed several groups at that time; however, he was not alone. The Keynotes, for example, played regularly in a Five Points upstairs restaurant (the current location of Saluda's) and booked their gigs primarily through Ray Sims, who lived on Laurel Street behind Benedict College. "Back then, Derrick would have a preshow [for] ninety-nine cents. School kids could go to a show, and then at night, the main show be at Township [Auditorium]... Charles Derrick started a lot of things in the '50s," Drink recalls.

Derrick helped to organize a major event at the Township Auditorium featuring Sam Cooke and the Soul Stirrers, the Swanee Quintet and the Spiritualaires. The entire auditorium was sold out. All of Drink's family and friends were there that night for his incredible debut. The performance was perfect, and the Spiritualaires were an instant success. Drink felt as if he were ten feet tall.

The event was successful despite the fact that the Township Auditorium was segregated like all public places in South Carolina in the 1950s. Black musicians from the major northern cities were often vocal about the hypocrisy of the situation. Sam Cooke was quoted as having said, "The one thing that stands out vividly in my brain was an auditorium we played, I believe it was in South Carolina, and the stage was in the middle—black on one side, whites on the other. You do what you gotta do, that's what you do."

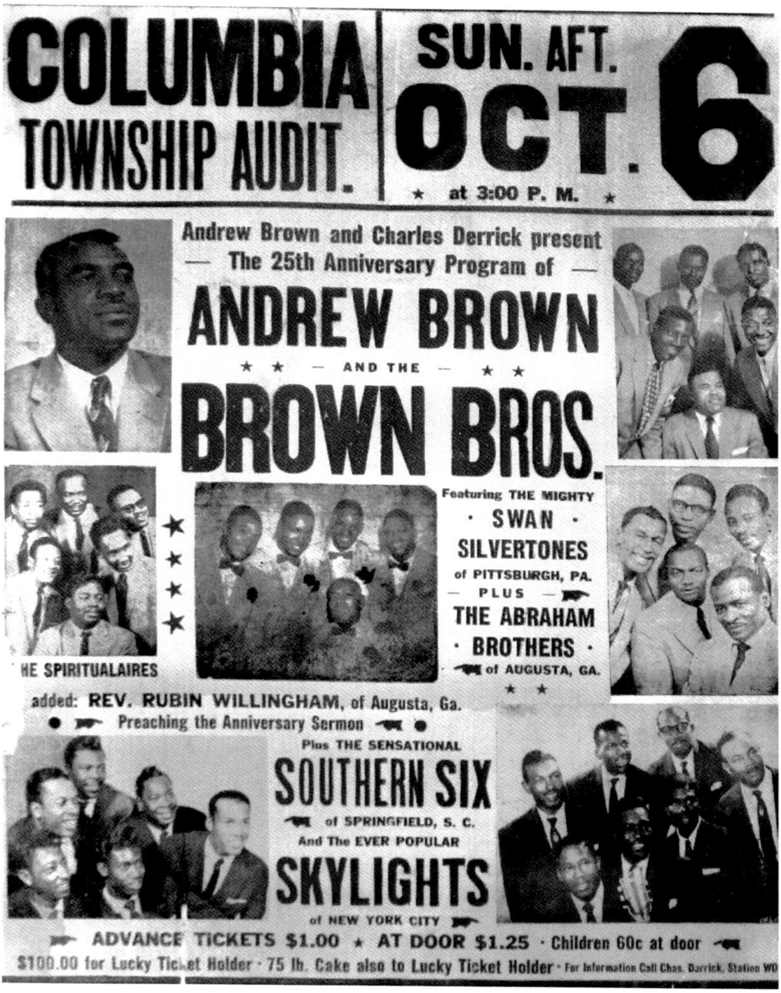


A Spiritualaires poster, circa 1957, Township Auditorium.

The Spiritualaires were considered to be a dynamic opening act and were in high demand. The success of the Spiritualaires allowed Drink to keep the promise he had made to his mother. Less than a year after he left Bishopville, Drink's beloved mother, Missy, moved in with Oma Jr. and Drink in Columbia in the Waverly neighborhood, which was an ideal fit for everyone's needs. Missy would not be alone, and she and Drink could walk to most places they needed to go. Columbia's historic Waverly community had a variety of African American–owned businesses affiliated with Benedict College and

Allen University, historically black higher education institutions founded in the late 1800s. Drink was familiar with both institutions and respected his classmates from Bishopville (Doretha Toney Gee, Ray Bradley, Eddie Isaac, James Lytch and Carrie Gass) who had chosen the academic path. Carrie Gass received a scholarship to attend Allen University, where she met Mary McLeod Bethune at the Township Auditorium. Carrie graduated, became a teacher at the Richard Carroll High School in Bamberg and went on to be the first African American teacher at Bamberg-Ehrhardt High School in 1967. Carrie dedicated her life to fulfilling Bethune's mission by serving as the founder and chairperson of the Committee for Progress and Understanding and becoming a member of the National Council for Negro Women (the nonprofit organization Bethune founded in 1935) and the National Association for the Advancement of Colored People (NAACP). She was also chosen as Allen University's Outstanding Alumni by the Lee County alumni chapter in 2004 and has maintained a friendship with Drink Small for over fifty years. Drink speaks highly of his friend and classmate, saying, "Now, she knows things. She's educated, traveled, made something out of her life." The Waverly community also had healthcare facilities, such as Benedict Hospital, the Evans Clinic and the Good Samaritan–Waverly Hospital, as well as physicians' offices on Hampton, Pine, Washington and Lady Streets.

Drink and Missy wanted to stay in the vibrant African American Waverly community. The house was close to the Greyhound bus station, a service Drink relied on. He explains, "I rode that Greyhound everywhere. Rode it so much I had to write a song about it. I wrote a song about riding the Greyhound bus—while I was riding the Greyhound bus!" Drink enjoyed traveling across the country: "Now when I was singing with the Spiritualaires, I got so many crisscross stuff. I been to Gary, Indiana; Milwaukee, Wisconsin—that was gospel. Topeka, Kansas—that was gospel. And St. Louis—that was gospel. Houston and Dallas, Texas—that was gospel with the Spiritualaires. And ah-and ah-now, Baton Rouge—that was gospel. They got a man there, Reverend Brown, he used to book the quartets in New Orleans." Drink was gaining national attention, and in 1957, he won *Metronome* magazine's "Best Gospel Guitarist of the Year" award. He was confident that his big break would be coming very soon.

Other gospel musicians had crossed over and were recording rhythm and blues songs because the genre had a broader audience and could lead to booking extensive concert tours. Some musicians had even abandoned their gospel roots to pursue secular music careers. It was 1957, and news that Sam

Cooke was recording secular music shocked the gospel community. To add to everyone's surprise, Cooke soon left the Soul Stirrers, considered to be one of the finest quartets of the era. Cooke's vocal style, lyrics and melodies had both crossover and commercial appeal. Drink never viewed this choice as abandonment, for he sees an emotional interconnection between the two genres. He explains, "Jesus had the blues. He had them because he didn't want the devil to get all of the souls. He turned the rocks to souls so the devil wouldn't get them all."

The music industry at that time inspired African American businessmen, women and individual artists to become more active in the business aspects of their work. Artists could clearly see that their music was making money; however, they were often not the recipients. Traditionally in the music industry during the late 1950s, white musicians would record a song that had originally been recorded and written by black artists. The copied version, or "cover," even if it was a lesser musical quality, was the song promoted by white disc jockeys and record companies. Certainly many of the early white rock-and-roll hits were covers of black rhythm and blues records that were popular on the much smaller black radio stations. The black music was taboo on most white-owned radio stations, but white artists and producers quickly saw and capitalized on white cover versions. Slowly, this trend began to change. White teenagers started seeking out the original recordings by black artists. Advertising sponsors and radio stations wanted to take advantage and capitalize on the growing market.

Drink, a deeply religious young man, was torn between his love for gospel music and his growing desire for success and recognition. All those years as a boy practicing the guitar, wanting nothing more than to be the best in Lee County, the best in Columbia—dare he say, the best in South Carolina. He knew plenty of guitar players and even better singers; he grew up with them. He had heard them perform in Columbia, and they were good, very good. Yet one by one, they began playing part time and eventually stopped performing. He was still playing. In fact, he was just getting started with his music career. He would not stop; he wanted to do it all. Drink decided that if he had his own group, he would have more flexibility to sing both gospel and secular music. Although he knew many talented musicians back in Lee County, getting them out of their small towns and persuading them to move or travel back and forth to Columbia was another story. Drink says, "I was playing gospel. I wasn't exposed to blues as much until I left Bishopville…I get Albert [Smith] to play with me, pull him out of the country, but he ducked me. Lord, he let me down. He was so country, he was scared, illiterate. He had that white people fear: 'Yes sir, yes sir.' Had that white people fear; he didn't fit."

Around this time, Kip Anderson, Drink's student musician friend from South Carolina State College, had transferred to Benedict College. After arriving in Columbia, Kip was approached by Barney Parks Jr., a former member of the gospel quartet the Dixie Hummingbirds. Parks was the manager and husband of Madame Edna Gallmon Cooke, a native of Columbia and a renowned gospel singer and recording artist from 1949 through the late 1960s. Madame Edna's regular pianist, Marjorie Cheeks, was often unavailable because she traveled with her husband, Reverend Julius Cheeks, who sang with the Sensational Nightingales and briefly with Sam Cooke when he was with the Soul Stirrers. In 1957, Cooke released his first number-one hit, "You Send Me." The ballad went on to pass Elvis's "Jailhouse Rock" on the charts. Parks hired Kip to accompany his wife from 1956 to 1957, and when this job ended, Kip was searching for another paying opportunity to help cover his college expenses. Drink reconnected with Kip. This was a match made in heaven because both Drink and Kip were serious about making music. Drink introduced Kip to Charles Derrick, and they worked on group and solo musical interests. Derrick introduced them to many popular stars of the day.

The Soul Stirrers toured nationally, playing sold-out concerts. Young musicians like Drink Small and Kip Anderson were also included in the impressive lineup. Musician Napoleon "Nappy" Brown of North Carolina was also Drink and Kip's friend. Napoleon had sung with the Bell Jubilees, the Southern Sisters, the Heavenly Lights and the Selah Jubilee Singers. Thermon Ruth, the gospel promoter from Newberry County who also sponsored the gospel music caravan tours, founded the Selah Jubilee Singers. Drink, Kip and Napoleon often performed at Columbia's Township Auditorium and numerous venues en route to New York's Apollo Theater in the late 1950s.

Drink was touring with the Spiritualaires, playing with his combo in Columbia and also caring for his mother. As exciting as this time was, it was a difficult pace to keep up. Alcohol and drugs were as much a part of the lifestyle as the music they played. Traveling with much older musicians exposed Drink to the best and the worst sides of his chosen profession.

As recognized as he was on the gospel circuit, Drink was not successful in getting his hometown radio station interested in his combo, nor could he compete with Jim Nesbitt in the mainstream clubs. Jim, two years older than Drink, was a popular white country western singer with a "talking cowboy" style. He was also Bishopville's local music hometown hero. Drink actually always appreciated good country music, explaining, "White people can beat black people in yodelin', black people can beat white people in moanin'...'I Can't Stop Loving You' was a country song, but Ray Charles did it funkier. It jus' like putting a little sugar in a cup of milk." He particularly enjoyed the WBT radio program *Arthur and the Cracker Jack* and even had the opportunity to play with Arthur Smith, North Carolina's bluegrass star. Drink now had mastered the Delta, Texas and Piedmont blues styles and had written hundreds of songs, although he did not write down lyrics or scores for any of the musical pieces. He had a different repertoire for each audience. If a song wasn't working, he would simply make up a new one on the spot.

Drink maintained a fan base in the African American community in his hometown of Bishopville and the surrounding counties. He was invited on numerous occasions to play in familiar places like the Davis Country Club on the outskirts of town and its new downtown location, the Davis Night Spot. On these visits back to Bishopville, Drink would often see his biological father, Arthur Jackson, at the club; however, there were few words spoken between the two men. To Drink, Arthur Jackson was just another partygoer there to drink, dance and pick up women. Drink was there to entertain, and the men rarely acknowledged each other.

Drink was not lacking for parental love and support. His mother made certain of that. Drink was very proud of how far he had come because his biological father had never traveled out of state, let alone visited prestigious venues such as the Regal Theater in Chicago; the Howard Theater in Washington, D.C.; and the Apollo Theater in New York.

Drink had found his place in an important era of American music history and wanted more. The 1940s and '50s have been called the Golden Age of Gospel, with male quartets and popular female soloists achieving stardom. The Spiritualaires of Columbia, with Drink Small as lead guitarist, were not overlooked. The group was hired by Thurman Ruth to perform at the Apollo Theater in New York with the Skylarks and Sensational Nightingales in 1957. Performing on the legendary stage was a tremendous thrill and the first of Drink's three trips to the Apollo Theater. While touring in New York City, Drink was one of many musicians who tried to find lodging at the Caesar's Hotel. The Hotel Theresa was known for being a cultural hub of black life in Harlem, but it was too expensive for anyone but headliners. There were always plenty of headliners, stars and celebrities staying at the posh hotel. Drink said, "When we get to New York, we are in Negro heaven! We would go across the street from Small's Paradise if we had to get our

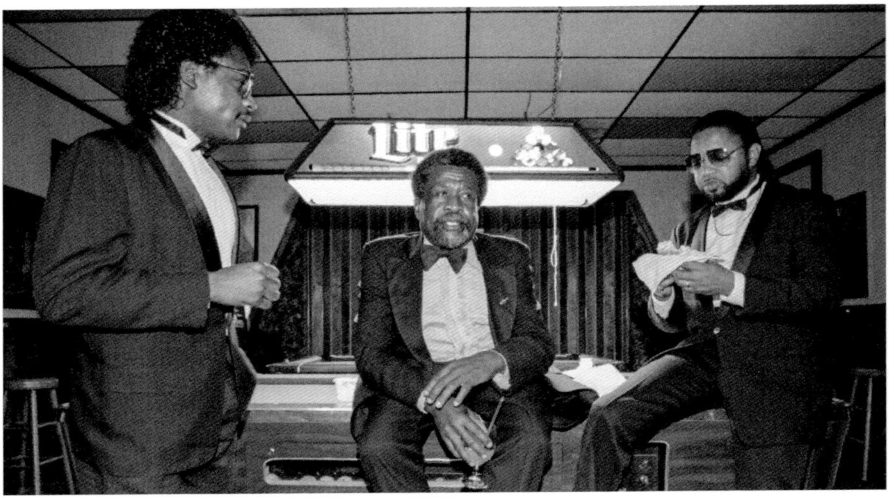


hair processed. The Caesar's Hotel had a jazz club downstairs, and all the old jazz guys would go jam. I was with the gospel group, but we would all go down to the bar and get a drink and catch the other musicians. I used to buy those jazz magazines [*Downbeat*]; I had two hundred of them. Strange guys would come in there. One night, an old trumpet player started to play. He got a way he approaching a song…The young guys run out of ideas. Song got to have simplicity. Jazz music you got a lot of strange notes; this old player knew where he was goin' with it. Later I remembered, this one of the cats I had read about in my *Downbeat* magazine!"

As much as Drink enjoyed traveling, he was never tempted to relocate to New York or Chicago like so many other musicians. "Plenty of interesting things about music in South Carolina and Columbia, too," he explains. "The Historical Commission, they try to keep the doors [of historic sites] open, but the people's eyes are closed. People just don't care about history like they should." Besides, South Carolina was his home. "My momma was there. No reason to go no place else. No, I wasn't leaving."

When he was back in Columbia and not touring, Drink could be found at the Rendezvous Café, about two doors up from the intersection of Millwood and Gervais Streets near the First Nazareth Baptist Church. If Drink was not in the café, he would be two or three blocks up the road in his little house in Liberty Hill Court, where the homes were clustered together with connecting alleyways. Drink made lifelong friends who spent time with him in his home, bought him a bottle of alcohol when he needed it and were always happy to drive him to WOIC any day of the week. Established and aspiring

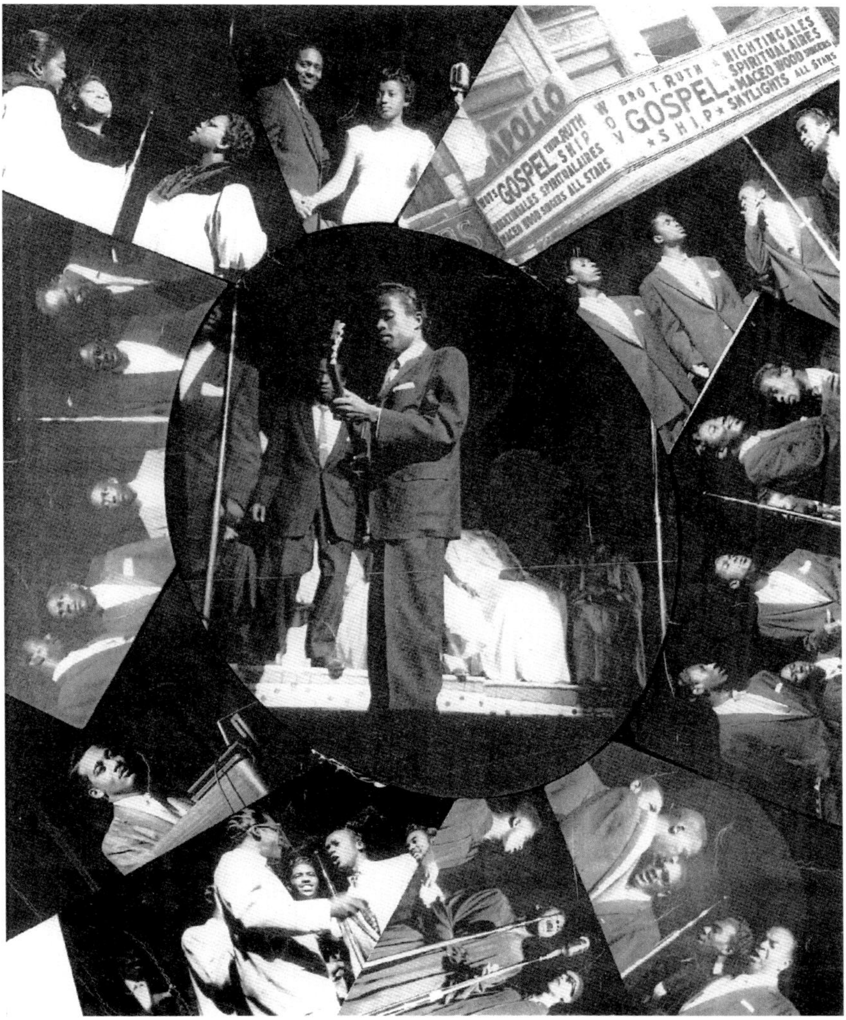


Apollo Theater, Drink Small with the Spiritualaires, 1957. *Courtesy of Drink Small, personal collection.*

*Opposite*: February 18, 1990 feature story by Elizabeth Lealand, Bob Leverone photographer. *Courtesy of the* Charlotte Observer.

musicians, politicians and local black business leaders all came through WOIC at one point looking to make connections of one sort or another. Bobby Smith was one of those individuals. Smith was a music industry pioneer from Macon, Georgia, and had started a small and often overlooked company named Confederate Records. In 1961, he had just recorded his new artist Otis Rushing and said, "Otis and I went on the road promoting 'Shout Bamalama.' Stopping at Augusta radio station WTHB, we were told by the deejay it would be played if it were taken off the Confederate-flagged record label. I promised to do so. We went on to Columbia, South Carolina, and met with a program director, Big Saul, at radio station WOIC, who also promised heavy play but only if the label was changed. Otis and I hit it off very well with Big Saul."

Saturday afternoons at WOIC often included spinning LPs, shooting dice, drinking a pint of Four Roses whiskey purchased from the liquor store near the trestle on North Main Street and harmonizing and writing songs. Hip deejays sent their cool signature tag lines over the airwaves. Charles "Big Saul" referred to songs by interesting names such as "oozin' music." He would also begin each show by saying something along the line of, "Here we are sitting on the banks of the Congaree, sipping our Kool-Aid and cruisin' on down the line." Big Saul was part of the legendary "Three Horsemen" of WIBB, along with Hamp "King Bee" Swain and Ray "Satellite Papa" Brown. Big Saul helped popularize rhythm and blues in the 1950s and early '60s, giving exposure to many up-and-coming musicians of the day, including James Brown and Little Richard. Originally a native of Jones County, Georgia, Big Saul played a critical role in the early stages of James Brown's career, according to news accounts. Charles Greene loaned James Brown $100 so that Brown and his band could perform some shows in Florida. When James Brown couldn't pay the money back, Big Saul convinced the owner of WIBB to allow James to record his song "Try Me" at the studio. Charles Greene paid $25 to get five records of the song pressed, and it became the singer's next hit. Charles Greene had been active in the civil rights movement and was fired from WIBB because he wrote a letter to the *Macon Telegraph* protesting the unfair treatment his wife received in a medical office. He remained active in the fight against discrimination while living in Columbia as well. Big Saul had a record store on Gervais Street where white and black youth convened to hear the latest hits. Teenagers from all socioeconomic backgrounds flocked to purchase the top charting records from the Harlem Hit Parade. The youth could also mingle with the popular WOIC deejays and artists, including Charles Derrick and Drink Small.

The magic being created within the walls at WOIC was capturing the ears of not only the white youth in town, but it rippled out to the county as well. Edward Manning was one of those early Drink Small fans. Ed grew up in Hopkins, on the outskirts of Columbia. His mother was a nurse for the elementary and junior high schools, and his father owned Manning's Grocery Store. He recalls:

> *The store operated from around 1952 through 1959 and was very busy. He* [my father] *put in a liquor store beside it, and my Great-uncle Tiff opened his semi-retirement doctor's office next door to it and provided medical care for anyone that needed it, and that included sharecroppers and domestics. The store was on Route #1 Hopkins. The post office then was by the railroad tracks next door to Mustard's Grocery, "Where Prices Are Born Not Raised"—interesting place...Buck Germany had another store just down the tracks, and it was Germany's Grocery. Black people were allowed to shop in all of the grocery stores in Hopkins. My father owned the largest store in that area, and he allowed credit, too. Mustard's Grocery, Germany's store and Davis's Grocery allowed all people to shop in their stores. Daddy's store had almost everything imaginable in it—it was the local hangout.*

Ed's father encouraged voter registration and voters' rights and assisted with the education of the local people in these areas. He was an advocate of being an informed voter and being encouraged, as well as allowed, to vote. The family experienced serious repercussions. According to Ed:

> *My father was beaten up at the polls in Hopkins by members of the Citizen's Council, a group of white people that were opposing integration and all components surrounding this. They had open meetings. Daddy refused to join them, and I think that they wanted to try and instill fear in him. The black people in our area were not in favor of integration at that time either. Ulysses Barber was the principal of the black schools in Hopkins and told Daddy, "I would not allow my daughters to go to school with some of the white trash here." These were very difficult and trying times, for many reasons.*

Ed was accustomed to seeing blacks and whites in the store, people who were friends and neighbors. At a young age, he remembers being at home dancing with his mother and father to records by black artists. He started his own record collection as soon as he was able. After high school, he attended the University of South Carolina, and that is when he first met Drink Small. He also attended the physician assistant program in Charleston. He is a physician assistant today and practices medicine in Alaska. "I know Drink won't remember me," he said, "but please let him know we will never, never forget him."

Like many college students, Ed was introduced to the music of Drink Small through the entertainment experts at SEMBO Enterprises, a band booking agency named after two Dreher High School student entrepreneurs, Sam E. McCuen and Bill Otis.

Dreher High School sits on the land that was at one time part of Wade Hampton's Millwood Plantation, and the school served the residents of the Forest Acres neighborhood. Sam's mother was a schoolteacher, and his father worked for Southern Bell. Bill's father owned the Columbia Lumber Company. Sam was a musician himself, a drummer, and had two bands: the Crimsons, so named because they wore red shirts, and the Royal Sultans. High school fraternities like the Dark Horseman and Esquire Club were famous for hosting popular parties with live bands. When they needed musicians for their parties, they turned to SEMBO Enterprises and other friends who spent time interacting with the African American musicians at WOIC.

While attending A.C. Flora High School, Harvey LeRoy "Lee" Atwater (political consultant and strategist to the Republican Party, advisor of U.S. presidents Ronald Reagan and George H.W. Bush and chairman of the Republican National Committee) loved James Brown, Wilson Pickett and Otis Redding. Lee had a reputation of being a high school bad boy. He was a member of the Dark Horseman, spent his lunch money on blues music and made sure that Columbia's rhythm and blues bands were booked and well received at A.C. Flora. Drink said, "I got a picture hanging on the wall: me, Derrick and Lee. Lee could play a guitar—oh yeah, he was good."

Lee bringing the bands to students certainly made him even more popular. Sam and Bill found a way to make it profitable. Derrick helped Sam meet and contract with the African American musicians who played the music the kids wanted to hear. Swing music was out; the white students wanted bands that looked and sounded like the Drifters and Little Richard.

There was plenty of work for all the bands, including Drink Small and his combo. Drink attracted young musicians, especially white guitar players who were enamored by his skill. He was invited to play with the boys and found himself a frequent visitor at the University of South Carolina. It was during this time that Drink met Sam McCuen and Bill Otis and started a formal partnership with SEMBO Enterprises. He said, "Sam and Bill, they the ones that got me started good with the college circuit." SEMBO musicians received 50 percent of the fee. SEMBO Enterprises would get 10

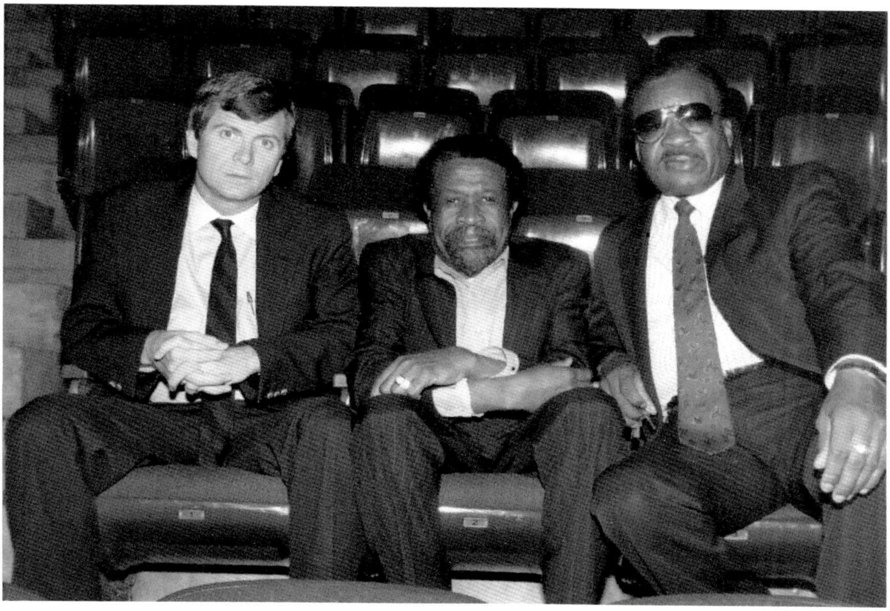

Lee Atwater, Drink Small and Charles Derrick, 1981, Columbia, South Carolina. *Courtesy of Drink Small, personal collection.*

percent from the client up front, and the balance was paid in cash the night of the performance during the intermission. SEMBO bands were in demand because Sam and Bill were very organized. They used formal contracts, had business cards and rehearsed their bands so every show was great.

The bands rehearsed in the Boy Scout club of the Eastminster Presbyterian Church on Trenholm Road. Drink was talented and also notoriously late for these rehearsals, although it was never his intention. Drink would promise Sam, "I swear for God to kill me, I'm gonna be there. I swear for God to kill me"—and Drink would still be late. Sam said, "If he wasn't late, it wasn't Drink." The music booking business became so popular that during Christmas and spring breaks, SEMBO would also book music for large hotels in the city like the former Jefferson and Columbia Hotel. They provided bands for the University of South Carolina in the years before the Student Union was booking entertainment; Columbia College; and private parties at the Columbia Women's Club located in Five Points. The bands played fraternity parties in the North Carolina mountains, as well as Myrtle Beach and the Pavilion on Pawleys Island. At one point, SEMBO had twelve

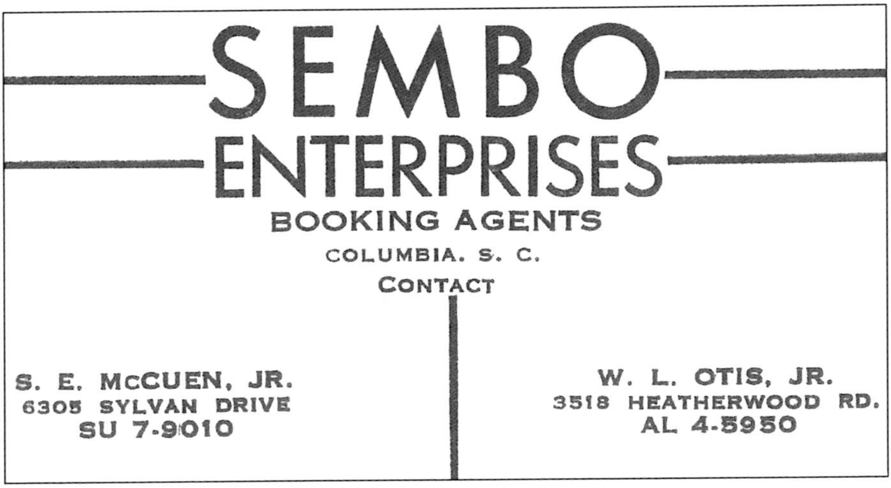
SEMBO
ENTERPRISES
BOOKING AGENTS
COLUMBIA. S. C.
CONTACT

S. E. McCUEN, JR.
6305 SYLVAN DRIVE
SU 7-9010

W. L. OTIS, JR.
3518 HEATHERWOOD RD.
AL 4-5950

A 1957 SEMBO business card. *Courtesy of Sam McCuen.*

to fifteen different bands on the roster. For Sam McCuen, the relationships with the musicians became true friendships. After all, Sam was a high school kid; he admired the older musicians and the younger ones, like Drink, who were just a few years older than him.

During the holiday season, Sam would give Christmas gifts to the bandleaders such as a necktie or other small item. One night while on an intermission break, Sam and one of the group leaders were outside in his car. They had parked in front of what was then the federal courthouse, behind city hall across from the former Jefferson Hotel. There was a knock on the window; it was a police officer. The officer assumed Sam needed help, but when he realized the two were actually friends, the officer chastised Sam for associating with "those people." The officer asked him when they planned on leaving and told him that he didn't want to see them hanging around anymore. Having African American musicians entertain at your party was one thing, but friendships between the musicians and white youth from "good families" was another thing altogether. Despite the racial tension of the time, Drink stayed focused on his music, playing and recording his own songs.

Derrick was very interested in managing Kip Anderson's career as a rhythm and blues artist and agreed to sponsor his first record. Kip had schoolbooks and college expenses to cover, so he was happy to also work on a group project with Drink. Drink, Kip, Howard Overton (playing drums) and Earle "Hambone" Cochran (on bass guitar) formed a combo and quickly became a Columbia and surrounding area favorite. The group was hired to play at the Hawaiian Stage Door and the New Club Cabana. Both locations had the same owner and catered to military personnel from Fort Jackson. These steady gigs paid well, with each musician earning fifteen dollars a night.

The combo also traveled to neighboring towns to play at other nightclubs on the weekends. Kip was writing songs in collaboration with a poet he had met at the Stage Door and had come up with a number of very good songs that Derrick thought could be real moneymakers. In 1959, Charles Derrick took Drink Small and Kip Anderson to Newark, New Jersey, to record original songs backed by professional musicians. They recorded with Herman Lubinsky on the Sharpe label, a subsidiary of Savoy Records. Drink recorded his first blues single, "I Love You, Alberta," which is considered a collector's item and a cult classic among blues fans. Kip recorded his debut single, "I Wanna Be the One," with a driving guitar solo played by Drink.

There were so many connections to be made in and around New York, and many of these individuals had roots in the South. The music business, especially among African Americans, was a small circle. If you looked hard enough, you were certain to find someone you knew. Ernest Kelly, originally from Orangeburg, had moved to New York. Kip had recorded one of the songs the combo played and gave it Ernest for distribution and promotion. The recording was called "Satisfied" and was on both sides of the record. It was produced by E. Kelly and released on Taffi Records in New York. The Taffi Record label credits the song as being performed by "Drink Small's Combo." Drink says, "I didn't know anything about that record. It was jus' somethin' Kip put together. He said, 'We gotta put somebody's name on, let's put Drink's on it.' The song played on the jukebox. It didn't go anywhere."

Ernest Kelly was recruited by Barry Gordy and worked as a writer and producer at Motown in Detroit, Michigan. In 1964, he released a soulful record on the prestigious Atlantic Records. The song was a soulful instrumental entitled "Satisfaction," performed by the Ernest Kelly Combo.

Just when it seemed like everything was falling in place for Drink, it suddenly seemed to be falling apart, at least for the Spiritualaires. Charles Derrick was unhappy with how Vee-Jay Records was promoting the group's single, and the Spiritualaires disbanded in 1959. This development was devastating to Drink. He was not one of the disgruntled members, nor did he get involved in disputes around who received credit for their recordings. The breakup of the popular group also worried Alice Small. The Spiritualaires were a religious group, and she believed that her son's life had been spared in the cotton field and therefore his musical talents must be used to glorify God. If he turned his eyes from the music of the church and set his sights on blues music, who knows what might happen to him. Missy confided in preachers and got everyone she knew to pray for Drink. He, on the other hand, took the Greyhound bus from town to town trying to earn a living.

In the spring of 1959, Sam McCuen was at Richland Custom Recording studio providing some technical assistance for Homer Fesberman, the studio engineer. A group of young men from Lancaster, South Carolina, was recording, and during a break, the band started improvising around a song they had written a few years earlier. Everyone loved its melody and catchy lyrics, so the band decided to record a quick demo record of the tune, which was then produced by Briarwood Enterprises. The group was Maurice Williams and the Zodiacs, and the song was simply entitled "Stay." Maurice Williams and the Zodiacs were getting a lot of interest in their latest song and were headed for a record deal. Drink was frustrated and confused, explaining, "All these musicians gettin' Cadillacs. I ain't got a scooter." Instead, Drink was forced to borrow money from friends to pay his rent. He had made many friends, that was certain; even parents of the white former high school students whom he played for were known to lend him a helping hand. The help was often a bitter reminder of the times, as when Sam McCuen approached a few of SEMBO's former clients to help out Drink. A woman who had known Drink for many years was delighted to help. Sam recalls she said in a very sincere manner, "How is Drink? Now that's a good Negro!"

Drink knew he was depending on the very people who would never have looked his way twice if it had not been for the music. He worked hard and kept his ears open and his mouth shut. While riding in the backseat of expensive cars, sometimes people forget you are there. "There are some things you just can't say you know. No, you can't tell it all," he says. Some fraternity parties required that he play until the early morning hours, yet the pay was inconsistent. Often he would get twenty-five dollars and all the alcohol he could drink, which was the type of arrangement Greenback made back in Bishopville. Drink started to raise and sell fishing worms from the backyard of the house on Lady Street. His frail and ailing mother begged him to return to gospel music. He recalls, "I was spinning round and round, but I wasn't going up."

Charles Derrick continued to promote Kip Anderson. Kip was touring as the opening act for Sam Cooke and Jackie Wilson. Kip relocated to Newark and continued to record and even make Billboard's top four. The single he had recorded on Derrick's label was re-recorded on the Checker label, a subsidiary of Chess Records, and went on to chart with singles he recorded at the Fame Studios in Muscle Shoals, Alabama. Drink recalls hearing Kip's song "I Want to Be the Only One" played on Nashville station WLAC. He says, "After the record ended, John R. [Richbourg], the wildly popular deejay and Manning, South Carolina native, said, 'I don't know who that was playing the guitar, but that was one of the best solos we've heard in a long time. That guitar got soul!' He was talking about me." Although Drink was recognized for his skill by one of the most important radio personalities of the time, no new recording contracts or deals came his way. And it was not long before Drink Small was once again looking for work.

Missy's cousin Rosa would come up from Bishopville on weekends to stay with her when Drink found a paying job that required overnight travel on Greyhound. He traveled through every county of the state, cities and small towns. Drink shared stories with people from all walks of life. Fairfield County residents have many memories of Drink. One consistent story was about an infamous party in the town of Winnsboro. The event was a going-away party for a young man who was headed off to fight in the Vietnam War and was held at a large private estate on Evans Street. Drink Small was the only entertainer for the entire event. Jimmy Burroughs was a young boy at the time and recalls:

> *I remember a story Willie Sherrod shared with me of riding in his mother's car. They drove past the house on Evans Street on Friday night, and the cars were parked everywhere with a line of people still driving into town. Willie's mother said, "What in the world is happening over there, William?" People still talk about that party to this day because everything you can imagine took place that weekend. There are rumors that Drink, like many of the other people, was found on the floor out cold. That was a long time ago, way before he got straight. Most of the people at the parties were all college kids or a little older. It was the '60s. Some are still alive; others are not. But that was the times, and that party was legendary! I always wish I'd been old enough to go to that party. Some of those people are judges and big-time state and national business leaders today. Everything you can think of took place in that house that weekend, and I tell ya, that party has tied Drink Small to Fairfield County forever.*

Drink's popularity among white youth continued to grow while racial tension came to a head. While he was playing music, many black youth at Allen University and Benedict College were focused on other causes

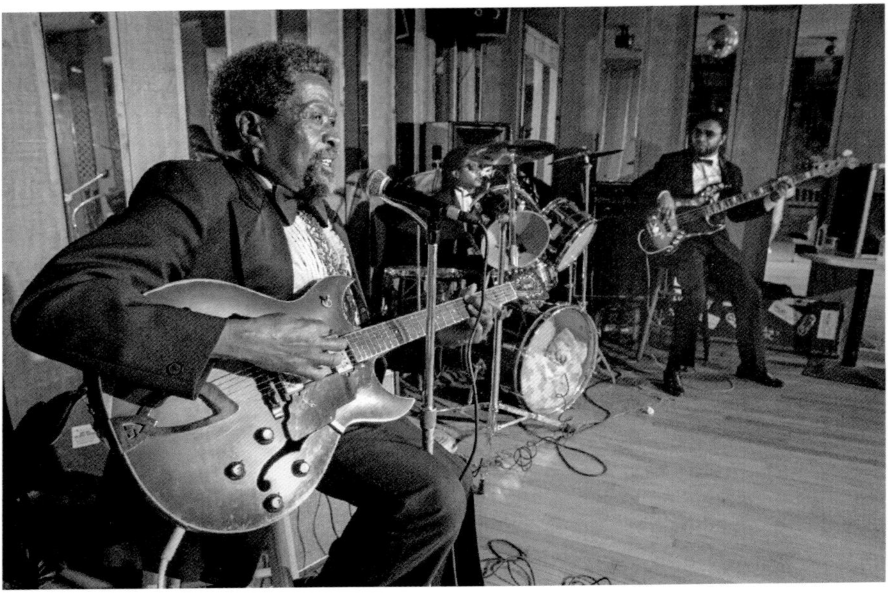

February 18, 1990 feature story by Elizabeth Lealand, Bob Leverone photographer. *Courtesy of the* Charlotte Observer.

altogether. Inspired by the "Greensboro Four," black students in South Carolina conducted sit-ins, marches and other acts of civil disobedience to dismantle segregation. Drink shared that there are still reminders of how far we have to go. He described a sign he saw just a few years ago painted on the side of a store that reads: "No niggers or dogs allowed." In March 1960, hundreds of black students from Allen and Benedict held a protest march to Main Street. Members of the WOIC staff were also active in Columbia's fight for civil rights. Reverend Bowman served as the state field director for the NAACP, organized sit-ins at segregated lunch counters downtown and facilitated workshops to teach people about the voting process. The protests and sit-ins resulted in the closure of stores such as Woolworth's and S.H. Kress. Drink knew the world around him was changing in many ways, and he didn't know exactly how or where he or his music fit in. Certainly the last thing he expected was that at age twenty-eight, he would become a father.

Glenn Anthony Miller was born on July 5, 1961. The relationship between Drink and the child's mother was almost nonexistent, and he has little to say about Beulah Mae (not her real name) Miller. No one has confirmed that

Beulah Mae was Drink's girlfriend or that the two were ever seen together at all. She was a local girl from a pious and religious family. Her father would never approve of a musician like Drink Small. The very fact that Beulah Mae had a baby was something her family would never accept. Drink, on the other hand, was excited about being a daddy. When he heard the news that Beulah Mae was in the hospital with a baby, he immediately called his old friend Sam McCuen to borrow the fifty dollars required to pay the hospital so that the baby could go home. Sam said, "He was really happy. I can't say she felt the same way at all. I don't know; the baby was drooling a lot and was not very alert. There was way too much drooling, you know, but Drink, he didn't seem to find that strange at all. He was holding the baby in his arms, proud as he could be." Once Beulah Mae left the hospital, Drink did not see the mother and child for some time. Nobody seemed to know what had happened to Beulah Mae Miller. Exactly eleven months later, Beulah Mae showed up at Drink's house. Her only words were that she was moving to New York City to become a hairdresser and could not keep the baby. She handed the infant to Drink and walked out the door. Drink Small and his aging mother now had a baby to raise. As hopeless as it all seemed, Drink refused to give up. With greater responsibility than ever before, he needed money, he needed gigs, he needed to get his life together and he needed his friends more than ever.

Sam McCuen was working as a reporter for the *State* newspaper and making a name for himself. On April 17, 1963, Sam interviewed Nation of Islam leader Malcolm X when he visited Columbia. With a promising career ahead of him, Sam was not playing music and had no need for his old drum set. Sam gave it to Drink for his combo. Drink told Sam he wanted to resurrect his career and get a record deal with a major label. Drink again began collaborating with Charles Derrick, but it was a slow process, he recalls: "Waiting for a record deal was like waiting to see Jesus come riding down Gervais Street with a Chesapeake dog and a blue-eyed monkey wearing a bow tie."

Things were tense at home, for the baby was an additional expense and responsibility that Oma Jr. was not prepared to take on. Joe Small convinced Oma Jr. to move up north, so he left South Carolina and found work in Brooklyn, New York. Uncle Louis had since left Bishopville, was married and was now also living in Columbia; he did what he could to help his sister, nephew and baby. Every door Drink believed might lead toward success seemed to close before he had a chance to go inside. He recalls, "This a rough place, trying to get people together around culture. We got too much discrimination, pol-la-tick-in', separation, you know? I was playing down in Charleston in the club, so I went to the radio station, to the deejay that had the blues program. I said, 'Hey man, I'm playing down here, got my record with me. Could y'all play that?' He say, 'Well, no, we don't play that black blues music. That's for the clubs, not the radio.'"

The late 1960s were bleak. The lot that Drink, Missy and the baby lived on had been sold by the landlord to the City of Columbia for the building of the Lyon Street Elementary School. Moving to a home without steady income was going to be difficult. Drink needed to find a place where they could stay for a long time. Affordable houses were becoming scarce because the neighborhood was growing as a result of the businesses and historic black colleges. With the growth seemed to come a renewed awareness that things for blacks in South Carolina were not getting better.

African American residents were extremely dissatisfied with the racial injustice they felt around them. WOIC's longtime black staff were not only dissatisfied, but they were also vocal and active. Drink looks back and says, "It was pretty bad. The deejays couldn't report the news they wanted. I didn't know Seidel [the station president], but I'd see him sometimes. Derrick, Bowman and those guys were mad." In 1968, Charles Derrick attended the first annual Billboard Radio Forum and made an impassioned speech about the racial prejudice he and other African American program directors were subject to. The speech was reported in the article "P.D. Derrick: Negro Gets Short Shirted" in the June 22 issue of the national music industry publication. Charles Derrick was popular with a large following. An integrated group of concerned citizens sought to support the predominantly black staff and demand better wages and fair employment practices. The station's owner and management refused to meet with the group, so the committee contacted the Federal Communications Commission (FCC) and requested that a study be conducted of the Columbia station. The group charged that the station refused to promote black employees to decision-making positions and their duties and responsibilities did not reflect their job titles.

The racial tension seemed to mirror the heat wave in the summer of 1968, as the temperature reached 102 degrees. Charles Derrick was focused on political issues, and Drink had little work from the promoter. The radio station was a controversial place to be, so Drink stayed away. Drink, Missy and the child rented a small, inexpensive home located at 2439 Lady Street, where they all resided for the next eighteen years. Growing up, Glenn Anthony was a very tall, large young man who didn't speak much at all. Every year around his birthday, he would receive a little money from the woman Drink told him was his mother. Drink could never understand Beulah Mae's decision to leave her child. His own mother never left or abandoned him, and his needs as a child were immense. Glenn Anthony seemed to have two very different personalities. The boy could be as kind as he was brooding and angry. But he was always very quiet and extremely neat. One individual described him as street smart. Drink and Missy appeased him. If cash that Drink had earned from his gigs went missing from the house, he would say, "Oh, well, let's jus let the boy be—his momma went off and left him…" And then Drink would borrow money until his next paid job came along. This became a way of existing in which he was trapped for many, many years.

In Columbia, Drink remained a regular part of the University of South Carolina campus. It became a home away from home. Drink always valued education, and he longed to be more like those fortunate young college students who could engage in stimulating debates and were exposed to the professors and scholars with impressive credentials and academic degrees. Drink had a thirst for knowledge and was well read, opinionated and preferred being around college students, intellectuals or serious musicians when given a chance. The doors to the university lecture hall seemed to be closed for him. He had a family to provide for, and for better or worse, he a bluesman. So Drink would spend hours at the university either performing, rapping about current affairs or relaxing with his young friends. Most of Drink's friends were musicians, and many continue to perform today all over the state and beyond.

Anderson, South Carolina musician Robert "Rob" Cassels recalls how Drink would come to his dorm room (the old "Honey Combs" Burney) and jam for hours on the guitar. It didn't take long before the small room was crowded with other young men eager to experience the blues. Rob said, "Drink played with real fat guitar strings back then, and he used to come to my dorm room and borrow my great big Kustom guitar amp. The amp was a Kustom 100, his guitar was an Epiphone electric hollow body… plugged straight into the amp." Rob also followed Drink around campus and accompanied him on the harp (harmonica). Rob said, "He used to tell stories in between his songs. He would say, 'Now B.B. King can play but ain't got my tone (Drink would play a wild chord on the guitar), and don't mis-con-strue me.'" Rob insists that he is a blues singer today because of Drink Small. Now Rob plays Christian blues and gospel, explaining, "I sound the way I do because of Drink. That was 1971. I don't know who named him Drink because I never saw him take a drink of nothing, not whiskey, nothing—but it's a good name, and he is a treasure."

Musicians from Columbia and the surrounding area colleges and even high schools found a tutor and mentor in Drink Small. Timothy Cromer is a musician who now resides in Miami and considers himself one of Drink's

West Columbia protégés. Even before Timothy found Drink, as a drummer he loved the African American high school bands that caught his ear and his heart. He said, "I started playing the drums as a kid. I remember those Thanksgiving and Christmas Day parades; I would sit on the corner listening to the bands. Then all of a sudden, here come the bands from C.A. Johnson and Booker T. You could hear those drums all the way up North Main. Here comes the Booker T. Tornadoes, and they were whipping ass! At eleven or twelve years old, I fell in love with the drums."

Timothy was introduced to Drink by a friend. Drink was looking for a drummer, someone who was good and also affordable. Tim said, "I just turned seventeen and was playing in a rock-and-roll cover band; now I was getting a chance to play with someone like Drink Small!" Timothy went on the road with Drink—on the dusty, backwoods road, that is. "We played juke joints out in the country. Little houses, outbuildings and shacks. I was the only white ass in there, but because I was there with Drink, I was loved on. I knew I was earning my badge." They traveled with an interesting cast of characters, including one in particular who Drink simply called the "vodka-drinking bass player." The juke joints and small clubs were a blast but soon gave way to bigger and better venues when a

> *blues promoter from Chicago heard about Drink Small and came down to Columbia to check him out. Jeff Schaffer knew he was hearing the real deal and adored Drink Small the man and musician. He booked us at the historic Great Southern Music Hall in Atlanta, and that was a gas! The trip over from Columbia was smiles and grins because this was a serious venue in my favorite southern city. Jeff had promoted and advertised, and the fruits of his labor was a packed theater. They fell in love with Drink's music and his inimitable wisdom and humor over the mic between songs. He was applauded like a star, and for good reason—he is! This event and my time with Drink remain a very fond memory in my musical journey. Drink was so very kind with his words and musical suggestions to this young seventeen-year-old drummer. I'm a better musician and a better man for my valued time in Drink Small's legions of musicians that have had the honor to back him up and be a part of his special magic.*

Today, Tim's band, High Gravity, plays regularly at Miami's historic Tobacco Road nightclub. In a recent phone conversation with Drink, Tim was sharing about his own band's upcoming gig: "I told him about playing with a really good blues-funk-rock ensemble down here [in Miami] and that, in fact, we were playing that night at historic Tobacco Road. He got all excited: 'Yeah, yeah, man, I know right where that is, on the Miami riverfront. I played that club many years ago!'" Timothy becomes very emotional when he speaks about Drink Small and says, "It was like 'full circle.' I just love that man."

Through the college circuit, Drink made a very important connection. He recalls, "I met a girl from Nashville, and she got me playing a lot of festivals, blues in the prisons, University of Tennessee. She was real heavy into the folklore part of it." There was a new appreciation for American roots music within regional and national arts organizations. As a blues musician, Drink benefited tremendously from this movement. "I was playing music, like I told Elfi [Elfi Lianna Hacker]—the Southern Arts Federation, that headquarter in Atlanta, that covered North Carolina, South Carolina, Louisiana, Virginia, West Virginia, Texas, Alabama, Mississippi, Arkansas. That cover the whole region and deal with southern culture, bluegrass and folk music and Peter, Paul and Mary, and you heard that man called Alan Lomax? Well, his sister named Bess Lomax Hawes, she the one that built Lomax Hall, and when I played Wolftrap Farm, she the one that take me to the bus station and come back to pick me up…Anne Romaine, that was her name, and Southern Grassroots Festival. Yeah, she was real big, so look her up, Anne Romaine…Look her up. And these are some of the people I worked with."

Anne Romaine was a folk music performer and historian and was active in the civil rights movement. Originally from Gastonia, North Carolina, she and Bernice Reagon (a SNCC Freedom Singer who leads Sweet Honey in the Rock) co-founded the Southern Folk Cultural Revival Project. The project presented traditional African American and white musicians in live performances together when it was unpopular to do so. The group organized tours throughout the South featuring roots and folk musicians, including Sparky Rucker, the Georgia Sea Island Singers, Nimrod Workman and others. Drink's involvement with the historically significant Southern Grassroots Music Tour in 1976 is documented and filed at Louis Round Wilson Special Collections Library at UNC–Chapel Hill and the David M. Rubinstein Rare Book and Manuscript Library at Duke University.

"I played all the prisons. That was called Arts for the Prisons. I played Rome, Georgia prison. A bunch of artists connected with the Arts Commission did the Southern Roots Heritage. You can try, but you never get it all down on me."

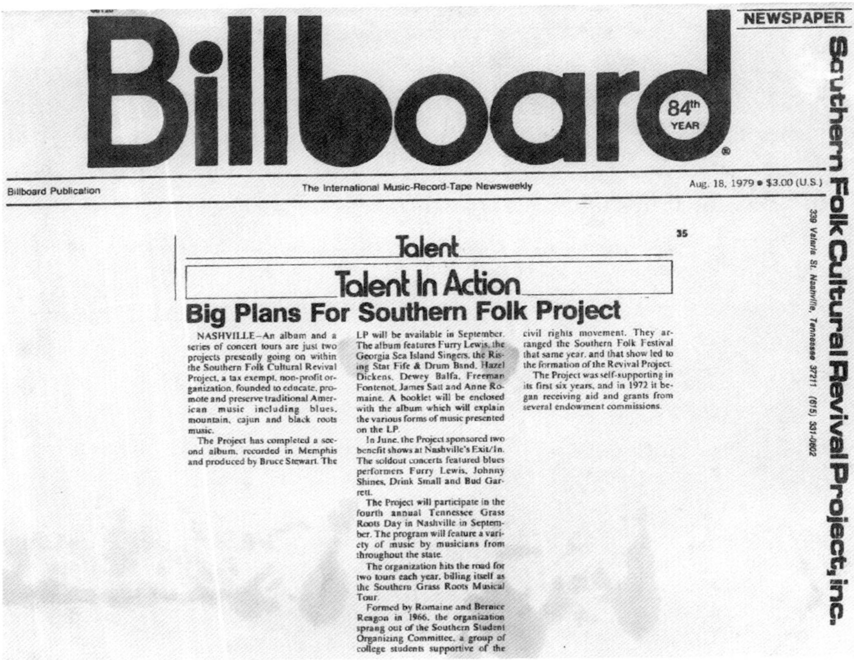

Billboard

NEWSPAPER

84th YEAR

Billboard Publication

The International Music-Record-Tape Newsweekly

Aug. 18, 1979 • $3.00 (U.S.)

Southern Folk Cultural Revival Project, inc.

339 Valeria St. Nashville, Tennessee 37211 (615) 331-0602

35

Talent

Talent In Action

**Big Plans For Southern Folk Project**

NASHVILLE—An album and a series of concert tours are just two projects presently going on within the Southern Folk Cultural Revival Project, a tax exempt, non-profit organization, founded to educate, promote and preserve traditional American music including blues, mountain, cajun and black roots music.

The Project has completed a second album, recorded in Memphis and produced by Bruce Stewart. The LP will be available in September. The album features Furry Lewis, the Georgia Sea Island Singers, the Rising Star Fife & Drum Band, Hazel Dickens, Dewey Balfa, Freeman Fontenot, James Satt and Anne Romaine. A booklet will be enclosed with the album which will explain the various forms of music presented on the LP.

In June, the Project sponsored two benefit shows at Nashville's Exit/In. The soldout concerts featured blues performers Furry Lewis, Johnny Shines, Drink Small and Bud Garrett.

The Project will participate in the fourth annual Tennessee Grass Roots Day in Nashville in September. The program will feature a variety of music by musicians from throughout the state.

The organization hits the road for two tours each year, billing itself as the Southern Grass Roots Musical Tour.

Formed by Romaine and Bernice Reagon in 1966, the organization sprang out of the Southern Student Organizing Committee, a group of college students supportive of the civil rights movement. They arranged the Southern Folk Festival that same year, and that show led to the formation of the Revival Project.

The Project was self-supporting in its first six years, and in 1972 it began receiving aid and grants from several endowment commissions.

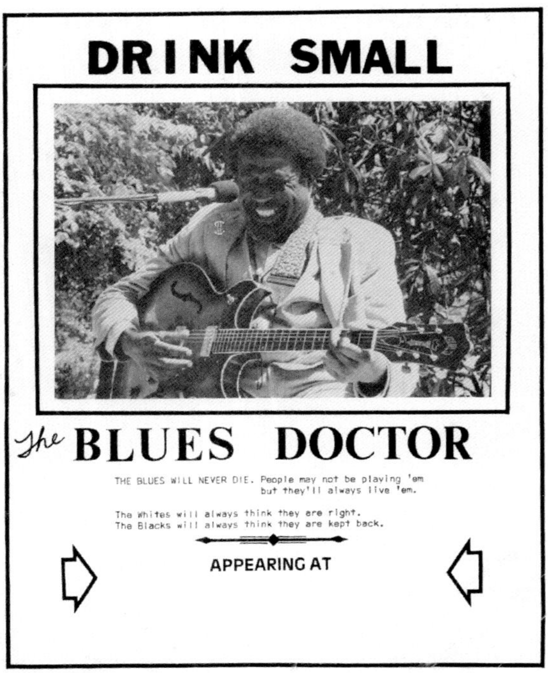


*Above*: A 1979 *Billboard* magazine article. *Courtesy of Drink Small, personal collection.*

*Left*: Drink Small's personal poster. *Courtesy of Drink Small, personal collection.*

However, in the unstable world of Drink Small, good things seemed to quickly evaporate right before his eyes. The good-paying club gigs ended, and the educational and cultural work ran dry. When he was without a manager, he would create his own flyers and beat the bushes for work.

Travel was hard for Drink. He didn't drive, and long trips on the bus could be physically uncomfortable. Occasionally, he experienced a sharp pain near his spine. Besides, his mother and his son needed him at home. Drink had to negotiate his own business deals, and truth be told, dealing long-distance with club owners was never easy, especially for Drink, who had a tendency to trust the wrong people too quickly. Drink Small was anything but naïve, yet out of necessity, he endured more than his share of humiliation and abuse. However, he was keenly aware that everything is not as it might appear to be.

## *Chapter 3*

# THE BLUES DOCTOR

In the early '70s, Drink was undoubtedly accomplished in so many styles of guitar playing. Although his signature fingerpicking was first rate, once again he was scratching and clawing, trying to get by. His life was a paradox, one part struggle and one part appointed keeper of the Piedmont blues. Many musicians wanted to imitate his style, but nobody wanted his life. He said, "What kind of job you got? You wanna trade yours for mine? I didn't think so." And that is the price he paid. All Drink wanted to do was make a living doing the one thing he excelled at. No matter how low he got, he refused to give up, although there were times when this required every ounce of strength he had.

Drink had been making calls for work, mailing out flyers and reaching out to every club owner he knew. After dozens of unreturned messages and, as he calls it, "the professional brush off," he received a call from a club owner in Pensacola, Florida. The gentleman, who had heard Drink play in South Carolina, wanted to feature Drink for a blues night at his club. Drink could play with the house band, so there was no need for him to bring other musicians. The club had a strong regular clientele who loved the blues. Drink would be the headliner, and it seemed to be a perfect gig, coming at just the right time.

Drink purchased a one-way Greyhound bus ticket to Pensacola, leaving early in the morning and traveling through the night. The club owner picked him up and drove him to the club, where had a bite to eat and chatted about the local blues scene. It didn't take long before the club was packed. Drink took the stage and played his heart out. He was having a great time, and the audience, of course, loved him.

As the night went on, Drink noticed the club owner was nowhere in sight. By the end of the second set, the audience was thinning. The third set ended, and Drink packed his guitar and waited. Soon the bar closed, and the band members started to leave as well. Still no club owner, and no one knew where he was or when he might return. Drink waited outside the club for another hour, but the owner never came back and Drink Small never got paid. Drink was stranded with no money for a ticket home, no place to sleep and nothing to eat.

He had to get home; his mother needed him. So with his guitar in one hand and his suitcase in the other, Drink hitched rides when somebody was kind enough to stop. When he had no ride, he walked, slept under bridges and sought out juke joints for hot meals. For the entire four-day trip, he thought a great deal about his life. Drink felt lost and completely alone—emotions that have been expressed by bluesmen and women for as long as there has been the blues.

*"Nobody Knows You When You're Down and Out"–Jimmy Cox*

*Once I lived the life of a millionaire, spending money, I didn't care*
*I carried my friends out for a good time, buying bootleg liquor, champagne and wine*
*When you begin to fall so low, I didn't have a friend and no place to go*
*In my pocket, not one penny. Friends? I haven't any.*
*So if I ever get my hands on a dollar again, I'm gonna hold on to it 'til them eagles grin…*
*'Cause nobody knows you when you're down and out.*

Once back home in South Carolina, Drink continued to visit WOIC. Things at the station were still not going well politically for Charles Derrick. The problems between the station owner, the African American staff and Concerned Citizens had really heated up into a very public legal battle. Drink doesn't recall how it all went down, but he said, "One day, Derrick went to the studio and there was a note taped on his office door. All it said was, 'This is to inform you that your services are no longer needed.' And that was pretty much the end of it all."

Charles Derrick's little office at WOIC had represented a world of opportunity and the possibility of success. Derrick always had multiple businesses going on. After twenty-five years with WOIC, he continued to promote select artists, direct a mass choir and operate a large commercial tour bus company. Charles Derrick also served as a field representative for Congressman Floyd Spence and Joe Wilson for thirty years.

As heartbreaking as it had been back in 1959, Drink never resented the fact that after the Spiritualaires folded, Charles Derrick chose to focus on Kip Anderson's solo career. There was nothing Drink would not have done for Kip; he had always been more like a brother. Although their musical careers had taken different paths, by the mid-70s, Drink Small and Kip Anderson were both living in Columbia and completely broke. Kip was battling a heroin addiction that had alienated him from the music industry. Kip had no place to live and bounced around from place to place, even spending more than a few nights sleeping under Drink's front porch. Drink was sympathetic; he knew firsthand how easy it was to lose your soul because the music business could drive you to do terrible things and go places you thought you would never go.

Being signed to a major record label didn't necessarily make life easier, he said: "You ain't no slave now, that's slave in another way…But don't ever sign your name with nobody putting big money out on you, 'cause when you feel bad, you gotta work when you feel bad…When they drop you, they can block you. They can make it so nobody else will hire you. It's best not to get into anything like that." Drink Small didn't turn his back on his friends, regardless of his circumstances.

Drink briefly enrolled in an accounting program at Midlands Technical College's Beltline campus. He said, "I was always trying to play music, but I was thinking I can make some money being a bookkeeper. In my class was a girl from India; she couldn't speak English. A couple of guys from the army in there. I got a kind of a mathematical mind, so I thought it be okay. But I didn't stay with it. I found out I'm not cut out for bookkeeping. I'm more like a poet; I like when the answer is something different every time! And that math thing? It was just too boring for me." Drink Small was anything but boring. He was not getting much work, and he certainly wasn't getting rich. However, in South Carolina, Drink Small was not just a bluesman. He was a single-handed entertainer and a bona fide personality.

The South Carolina Arts Commission (SCAC) had grants and resources to support regional visual and performing artists. The organization eagerly assisted Drink in booking festivals and in the production of several albums, including his 1975 hit "I'm Gonna Shag My Blues Away." Drink said, "It sad that many young blacks in South Carolina reject beach music and shag because they think the music has white-only roots…Joe Pinner, when I did 'Shag My Blues Away,' he got me coming to ten-ten [WISTV] back down

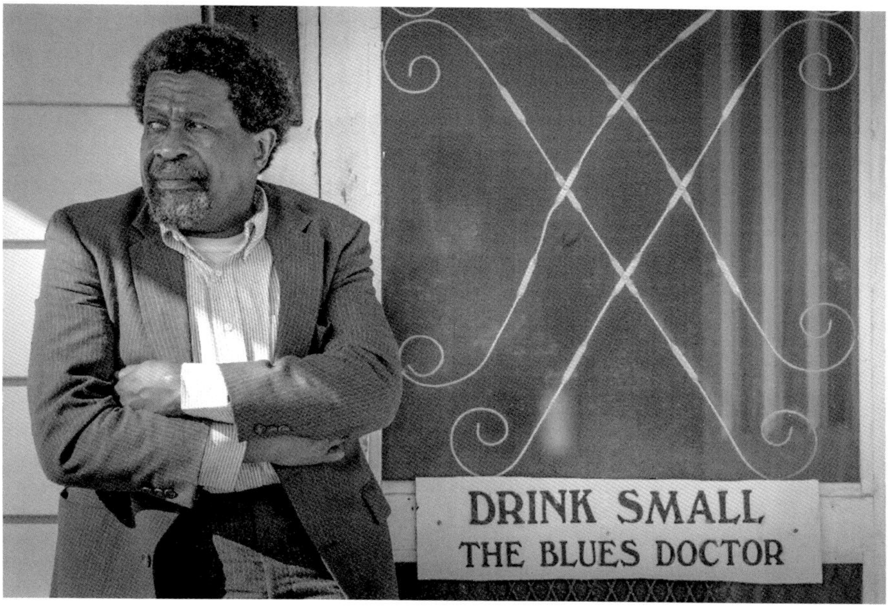


February 18, 1990 feature story by Elizabeth Lealand, Bob Leverone photographer. *Courtesy of the* Charlotte Observer.

there on Gervais Street. I played the first Spoleto and many more of 'em. The first time it came here, I played it…I played around Charleston fifty years."

The South Carolina Arts Commission was an important part of Drink's creative network, he said: "Some producers and sponsors don't care about the musicians; they just work 'em like a mule. The Arts Commission people care. They were always so good to work for. You could tell they cared."

In 1977, his longtime friend Kip Anderson was sentenced to ten years in Columbia's Central Correctional Institution. Drink had seen too many musicians lose the battle and said, "They smoke joints, do all kinds of drugs, always getting high. You see at the break, they gotta go out back and then come back talking funny. Musicians been doing that for years. A lot of them died young too; you can count the ones get seventy years old…Now you watch that, you never get old listening to young people."

Drink kept working the small clubs throughout the state. Some gigs were better than others. Some paid well, while others paid barely enough to cover expenses. Yet he didn't treat them any differently, and that's what fans could always count on: Drink Small gave them everything he had.

*Letter from One Drink Small Fan to Another:*
*Read at a reception honoring Drink at the 2014 Clemson Blues Festival*

*Paul,*

*If you get to speak with Drink Small, tell him a friend of yours from Bishopville regrets missing him.*

*Back in the 60's and early 70's, country music and beach music were the big things in Bishopville. If you only listened to WAGS (the local AM station), you would have thought the Tams and the Georgia Prophets were as big as the Beatles. Jim Nesbitt was the local country music hometown hero.*

*Every once and awhile, I heard the name Drink Small mentioned but never heard his music or saw him perform. If he did play in town, it wouldn't be where a white teenage kid could see him. There were a couple of joints in town like Davis Night Spot or Davis Country Club where he may have played, but those were black clubs that I'm not sure I could have entered.*

*In 1978 (or '79), I heard that Drink Small would be performing at the first Lee County Cotton Festival and decided to come home from college to check it out. I brought a friend who was from New York home with me. John had not experienced the rural South, had never seen cotton fields, and sure hadn't seen anything like Drink Small.*

*Almost all of the Cotton Festival activities were taking place on the edge of town, in front of the Armory, but Drink was relegated to the other side of town, on a backstreet loading dock where the fertilizer trains would unload. It was a hardscrabble, gritty setting which suited Drink's music perfectly. He was sitting on his amp, hunched over his guitar, growling and pouring the music out. There were a couple of winos shuffling around and maybe 20 people there in total. My friend John and I were the only white faces. It was an almost euphoric experience for both of us. There was nothing slick or pretty about Drink and his 2 piece band, but this was what the blues were about and how they should sound.*

*Please wish him well for me,*

*Mark W. Payne*
*Greenville, SC*

Drink's reputation continued to grow in his home state, and as the college kids moved on with their lives and careers, they carried their admiration for the Blues Doctor with them. Meanwhile, back at Savoy Records, Nappy Brown had experienced a resurgence in Europe in the 1980s. Drink was never comfortable with the idea of flying; he was not as much afraid as he was superstitious. He received offers from festivals and European event

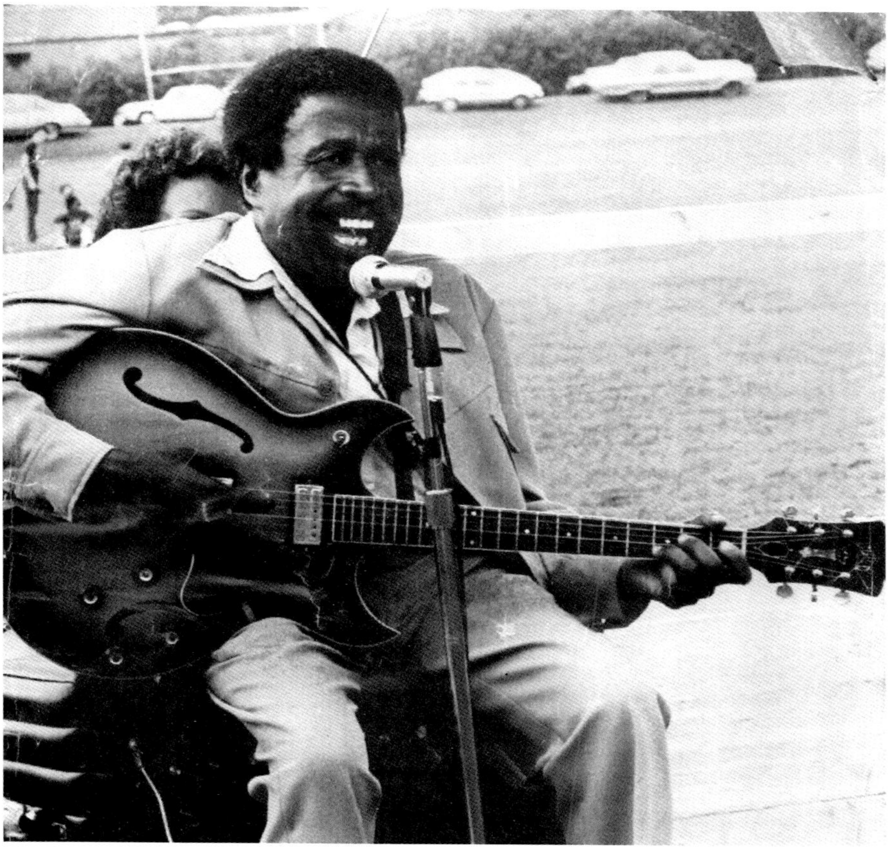

A World's Fair flyer. *Courtesy of Drink Small, personal collection.*

promoters on a regular basis, but he chose to stay regional. Certainly his mother's health was always a primary concern.

Along with festivals and educational concerts in the early '80s, he notes, "a fellow from Atlanta, Georgia—he was in charge of some of the World's Fairs—he got me to play in Knoxville, Tennessee, in '82, and I believe that was '84, he got me to New Orleans. He the one that set those things up. That where I met Robert Lockwood, Sparky Rucker…he deep in that too. I was gettin' all them awh-wards, but I wasn't gettin' any rhee-wards."

From 1977 to 1985 Drink, became a regular guest on Jimmy Burroughs's radio program, *Big Boss Man*. Jimmy found out that Drink resided on Lady Street in Columbia and went down unannounced. There was a sign on the door that read "Drink Small, the Blues Doctor." Drink tried to show Jimmy a few guitar licks, and Jimmy recalled how Drink would tell him, "Boy, you can't play the blues until you lived the blues. Blues is a feeling." When the WCXM radio show ended, Drink gave Burroughs a Gibson guitar, which he signed.

After the radio show ended, Jimmy Burroughs was serving as the Winnsboro chief of police. He would still put the Gibson in the car, ride down to Columbia and spend time with his "dad" (nickname for Drink). Drink continued to struggle financially and was raising fishing worms in the backyard to earn extra money as he was taking care of his mother. Drink was committed to being home with her as much as possible. He was often seen pushing Alice in her wheelchair to her doctors' appointments and the store and hitching rides with friends to run necessary errands. He was also experiencing his own health issues. Drink was having trouble walking, and his vision was starting to blur. "Blindness in my family, it hereditary. I got two aunts went blind in their seventies. If something hereditary, there ain't nothing a doctor can do…It hereditary that mean it a part of you, am I right? Well…all right then." With no health insurance or regular income, Drink ignored early warning signs. Although he had been eligible for Social Security, he was afraid to fill out the forms because he thought they would put him in jail for lack of payment of taxes. Jimmy Burroughs drove down from Winnsboro to take Drink to the Social Security office in Columbia and helped him complete the paperwork. When it came to income tax and finances, Drink had really been taken advantage of by some of his early managers, promoters and club owners. He had very little materially to show for decades of work, although his name was a popular draw for festivals and club owners. "I'm blind, I'm broke, got nothin' in the pocketbook, and I been used by a whole lot of crooks. Now write that down in the book."

The name "Drink Small" continued to draw crowds at clubs around the state. Drink shared how a defunct local club owner offered to give him a birthday party. The event turned out to be less of a party and more of a way for the club owner to fill his establishment by promoting the event as a Drink Small concert. Drink was told he could have a VIP table for friends and dinner for his musicians. That January evening, the restaurant was packed; however, there was no singing of "Happy Birthday," no banner, no cake, not even a card. Drink performed on stage as promised, and at the end of the night, the club owner handed Drink a bill for $175. An outraged family member went back to complain, and the club owner barely looked up from the register as he counted the night's receipts and barked, "F--- Drink Small." Drink paid the musicians with the money left in the tip jar on the stage.

Drink explained, "Sometimes I play for a benefit or they end up slow night, bad weather. I say to the owner, 'No problem, man, you hit me next time.' But some of those guys that used to play with me, call themselves my friends, they don't care. They see we ain't get paid, but they want theirs on the spot. You know Armond Dugan [not his real name]? He knowed me for what, fifty years? Every time he plays with me, he gotta be paid! He ain't never said, 'That okay, man, I see they ain't no money tonight.' And been in my house a hundred times; I ain't never been invited to his house, don't even know where he live. But he'll tell everyone, 'Oh, Drink Small? Yeah, he my good friend.'" Friendship is something that Drink Small takes very seriously.

In 1987, his friend Kip Anderson had served his time and was playing and singing gospel music, which he released on his own record label. The two men continued to say in contact while Drink worked statewide and regionally. The years on the road, club scene and party life had taken a toll on them both. Drink's superstitious nature also extended to doctors and hospitals. He refused to go to the doctor about his ongoing pain, discomforts and now occasional breathing problems. His eyesight was seriously starting to fail.

Although at this time Drink was not being managed by Charles Derrick or Sam McCuen, they remained in communication, always looking for that opportunity that might put Drink on the map. However, the industry was changing. CDs were now the new thing, and every musician needed to have one.

While Drink was performing at an event in Charleston, he was introduced to a talented promoter, producer and musician who was working hard to create a vibrant blues scene in South Carolina. Drink had been around for a long time, and he knew that to get something going in South Carolina was no easy task. It would require a love of the blues, talent, intelligence, contacts and a great deal of business finesse. Drink's new friend and future business partner was just the man for the job. After all, they don't call him Shrimp City Slim for nothing.

Gary Erwin started playing blues on the radio in 1984 and also had a blues program on public radio for seventeen years. He worked extensively with many blues artists and released albums by Drink and others. He was able to book a string of gigs for Drink throughout the Northeast, and they traveled to major festivals and concert venues in Massachusetts and Chicago. Drink had not had anyone this committed to his career for so long, and he was grateful for the help. Gary was sensitive to Drink's commitment to his mother and tried to coordinate a touring schedule that would accommodate Drink's needs to be home. Gary knew that if he could just get Drink to the people, Drink Small, the Blues Doctor, would always deliver.

The 1988 album *The Blues Doctor Live & Outrageous!* was considered by blues historians the ultimate Drink Small album with marvelous guitar work. The album was nominated for a prestigious W.C. Handy Award. Gary had high hopes that he could help leverage the prestigious honor and finally crack open some major doors for Drink. In some national professional blues music circles, the album was being touted as a blues masterpiece. Drink Small was hailed as the South Carolina real-deal bluesman.

In July 1989, Drink was not touring. It had been an extremely hot summer. Drink was at home with his mother, who was not feeling particularly well. Drink remembers trying to redirect the electric fan so it was pointed directly on her and trying to make her as comfortable as possible. She was sweating so badly that he knew he had to get her to the hospital. Frantically, Drink started to make calls to his friends for help. He called Charles Derrick and asked him to please pick them up because he wanted to get his mother to the hospital. Derrick arrived as quickly as he could and drove Drink and Missy to the emergency room at Richland Hospital. Drink remembers that the waiting room was extremely crowded, with long lines at the counter and people sitting in every chair. He ran and got a nurse and put his unstable mother in a wheelchair so she could rest while he filled out the paperwork standing right next to her. He said, "A lot of people knew me; they kept coming up to talk to me. I heard my momma sort of cough like choke, and when I turned to look at her, she dropped her head. I was yelling, 'Come quick, I need help.' The nurses run other, they call for some other…what you call 'em? Then they brought out one of them rolling beds and put her on it and took her away."

A few minutes later, Drink was informed that his mother had died while seated in the wheelchair, and they asked him what he would like them to do with the body. Drink was in shock and unable to speak. Charles Derrick took over and made the necessary phone calls and all the arrangements. The only thing Drink could say was that his mother had to be buried at home. She had to go back to Bishopville.

The body was picked up, and Charles Derrick continued to oversee the situation, which was simply more than Drink could handle. Drink said, "I didn't even know how old she was 'til she was funeralized at Square Deal Funeral Home in Bishopville in 1989." For months after her death, Drink reflected on his life and the dreams he once had, not only for himself but also for his mother. He had been so proud when he brought Missy to Columbia from Bishopville. He had envisioned them living the good life together, her son a successful recording artist, her without a care in the world. What had he done wrong? Sitting in the house on Lady Street, it was clear that nothing had turned out the way he had planned. Drink Small sunk deep into despair.

*"Wasted Life Blues"—Bessie Smith*

*I've lived a life but nothin' I gained*
*Each day I'm full of sorrow and pain*
*No one seems to care enough for me*
*To give me a word of sympathy*
*Oh me! Oh my! Wonder what will the end be?*
*Oh me! Oh my! Wonder what become of poor me.*
*No father to guide me, no mother to care*
*Must bear my troubles all alone*
*Not even a brother to help me share*
*This burden I must bear alone*
*Oh me! Oh my! Wonder what will my end be?*
*Oh me! Oh my! Wonder what will become of poor me.*
*I'm sittin' and thinkin' of the days gone by*
*They fills my heart with pain*
*I'm too week to stand and too strong to cry*
*But I'm fore getting' it all in vain*
*Oh me! Oh my! Wonder what will my end be?*
*Oh me! Oh my! Wonder will become of poor me*
*I've traveled and wandered almost everywhere*
*To get a little joy from life*
*Still I've gained nothin' but wars and despair*
*Still strugglin' in this world of strife*
*Oh me! Oh my! Wonder what will my end be?*
*Oh me! Oh my! Wonder what will become of poor me*

Drink continued to live in his house with his son. He loved his son a great deal, but they had an unusual relationship. This was such a difficult time for both of them. Drink, still noticeably depressed, did not care how the house looked. He piled books and old newspapers in the corners of the rooms. Glenn Anthony was moody and sometimes angry. The conversation between them was minimal and often strained. Drink was not working, and with less money in the house, things started to disappear. There were so many people coming and going, and Drink just did not have the energy to care. Glenn Anthony found an outlet at

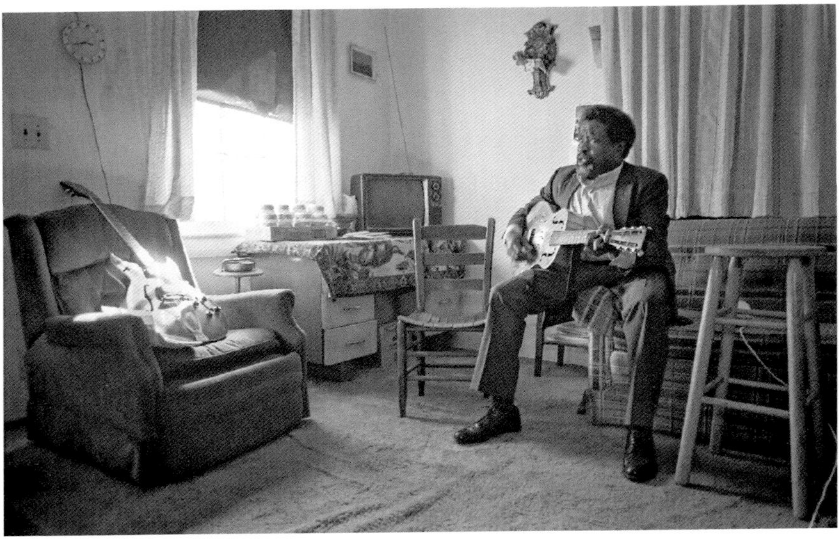

Drink playing guitar in the house on Lady Street. *Courtesy of the* Charlotte Observer.

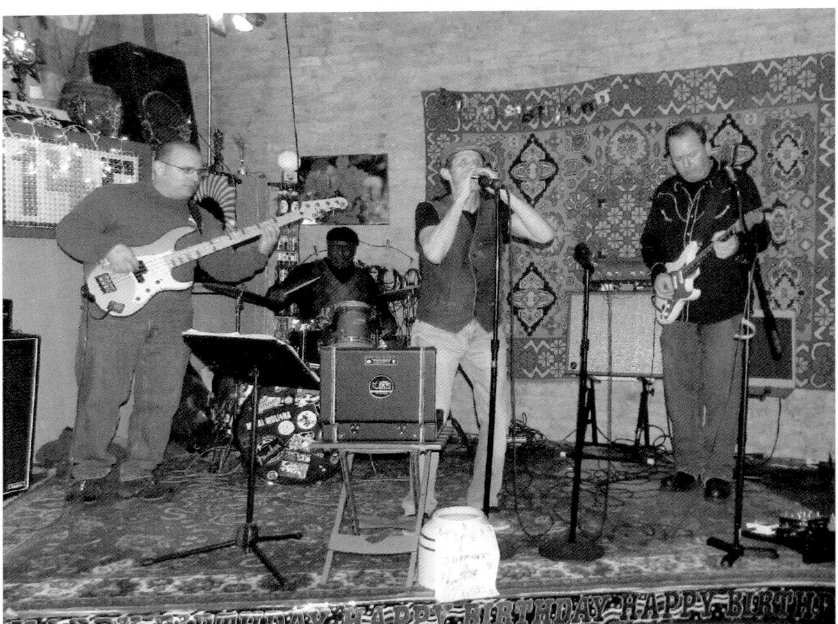


Anthony Charles and the Blues Dolphins (Mark Sobus at left, John Hartness at right and James Casey on drums) perform at the 145 Club for Drink's eighty-first birthday. *Courtesy of Elfi Hacker.*

work. He was a faithful and well-liked cook at the University of South Carolina's Capstone restaurant.

One day, a family friend was surprised to find a street vendor selling brand-new Drink Small CDs. When he asked the seller where he got them from, he simply stated that some guy had sold him a whole box of them for twenty dollars. Drink was grieving; he couldn't keep up with it all.

One year after Drink lost his mother, he received true recognition from his home state. In 1990, South Carolina honored Drink Small with the Jean Laney Harris Folk Heritage Award, the state's highest award for lifetime achievement in the traditional arts. This did a lot to lift his spirits.

Drink Small was part of the very fabric of Columbia. Bob Coble was elected mayor of Columbia in 1990 and served until 2010, and he often invited Drink Small to perform at his campaign events at his headquarters on Ott Street. Also in the fall of 2010, when Michael Steel came to South Carolina as part of his "Fire Pelosi" bus tour, Drink Small entertained at the University of South Carolina during the Columbia stop. Drink Small's brand of the blues was about as bipartisan as you could get.

Drink was still residing at 2349 Lady Street in the Liberty Hill Court neighborhood and was performing regularly in the Greater Columbia area. It was not uncommon to pick up the *State* paper to read about the area nightlife and see Drink's name on a weekly basis. Bill McDonald, who wrote for the entertainment section in the paper, said, "I wrote about Drink consistently, covering his performances around the state from 1970 through the '90s." Between the South Carolina Arts Commission, Charleston cultural events, tourist season at Myrtle Beach and Upcountry festivals, Drink worked and had a wide variety of musicians who would accompany and befriend him. Many of these musicians continue to keep in touch, visit or call. All of them benefited from their time with Drink Small. He refers to them as his "blues children."

## Stories from a Few of Drink's Blues Children

### *Scott Perry, Floyd County, Virginia*

Scott Perry currently resides in Floyd County, Virginia, where he lives with his family on their forty-acre farm. Perry is a solo artist and also has a band,

Front Porch Swing, known for playing traditional and original acoustic blues, jazz, honkytonk and vintage rock-and-roll. In a blog entry on his website, he shared his story about time spent with Small: "I've had the opportunity to meet and trade licks with a number of the 'living legends' of the blues over the years. Every visit or jam session has a fond memory attached to it, and most encounters left me with a good story to tell. However, if I had to choose my most memorable encounter, I'd have to choose the first time I met Columbia, SC bluesman Drink Small, the Blues Doctor." Perry shares how he met Small around 1993 while doing some work with a Blues in the Schools program. Perry served as Drink's ride and guide for the multi-week program that would teach high school–aged children about blues music. As Perry drove Small from school to school, they spoke about everything from current events to guitars to women.

> *We were hitting it off pretty good and somehow or another I got the bright idea that I'd tell Drink that I played and sang some blues as well. "Really," Drink said with a bemused chuckle. "I'd like to hear some of that!" That seemingly innocuous statement was to earn me a big ol' heapin' helpin' of humble pie before day's end.*
>
> *By the end of the school day, Drink had lit up several school auditoriums with his singing, guitar and piano playing. Oftentimes there was no PA provided for his performance, yet he demonstrated a supernatural ability to fill a room with his deep baritone and funky playing. All the kids loved him, and I was often forced to drag him away from a group of new (and many old) adoring fans so we'd make it to the next presentation on time. As we headed toward his home, he seemed very satisfied with how things had gone on his first day, but he quickly turned his attention to more mundane matters. You see, Drink don't drive, and having access to wheels and a willing driver provided him with the opportunity to "get some things done." Before I knew it, I was wheeling all over Columbia so Drink could pay bills, pick up laundry, buy groceries and complete assorted other chores. When we were finally headed toward Drink's home, I was just a bit put out at having been coerced to be his chauffeur for the last several hours, especially since I still had a two-hour drive home to Charleston ahead of me.*
>
> *As we pulled in front of Drink's home, I said my goodbyes as pleasantly as I could, given my current state of mind. "Where you goin'?" Drink asked. "You got to come on in and show me some of that blues you play." I made several attempts to explain that it was late, I was hungry and I had a family to get back to, but Drink was having none of it. "Come on now,"*

*he said. "You got time to play me one song." After a few more attempts at making an exit, I finally relented, figuring that it would take less time to play a song than to convince him I didn't have time to do it. We entered Drink's home, and he motioned me to a chair while he sat across from me and reached behind himself for his guitar. As he handed it to me, I could see that this box was a real "beater." The rusty strings were raised so high off the fretboard that you could about fit your hand between them. "Here, boy," Drink challenged. "Play me somethin'." I looked at the guitar again, cradling it in my lap as I attempted to fret a few notes. "I don't know, Drink," I said. "This guitar's in pretty rough shape." "Ain't nothin' wrong with that gitah," Drink retorted. "You go and play me somethin'. You do play, don't you?"*

*It probably had a lot to do with my being put out by hauling him all over creation, but there was something in Drink's tone now that really got under my skin. "All right, you cranky old man," I thought to myself. "I'll show you some playing!" I decided that I'd whip my "showpiece tune" on ol' Drink and really show him what I had and launched into Mississippi John Hurt's "Candyman."*

*Now, for those of you unfamiliar with guitar playing or this particular tune, it begins with a sort of fancy fingerpicking lick way up the neck of the guitar by the twelfth fret. Remember how I said the action on this guitar was so high you could fit your hand between the strings? Well, that was at the first fret. Way down at the twelfth fret, you could practically turn your hand sideways without touching!*

*As you can imagine, playing my most challenging piece on this old plank (which also went completely out of tune when I tried to force the strings down) came across pretty badly. Being angry and mule headed, I forced myself through the tune and, despite the cool weather, broke into a frustrated sweat while I croaked out the raunchy lyrics and wrestled with that unruly guitar. When I finished the piece I was sweating and visibly frustrated. I handed the guitar back to Drink, and he nodded his head and said, "Well, boy, that's some kinda playin'. But you ain't really playin' the blues now. You're usin' too many fingers."*

*I stared at Drink incredulously for a moment before I exploded. "What in the hell are you talkin' about, Drink! Nobody could make that guitar sound good, not even if they played it with twelve fingers!"*

*Drink chuckled softly and said, "Now there ain't a thing wrong with this ol' guitah. All you got to do is know how to play it. You see," he said, holding up his right hand and wiggling his thumb and first three fingers,*

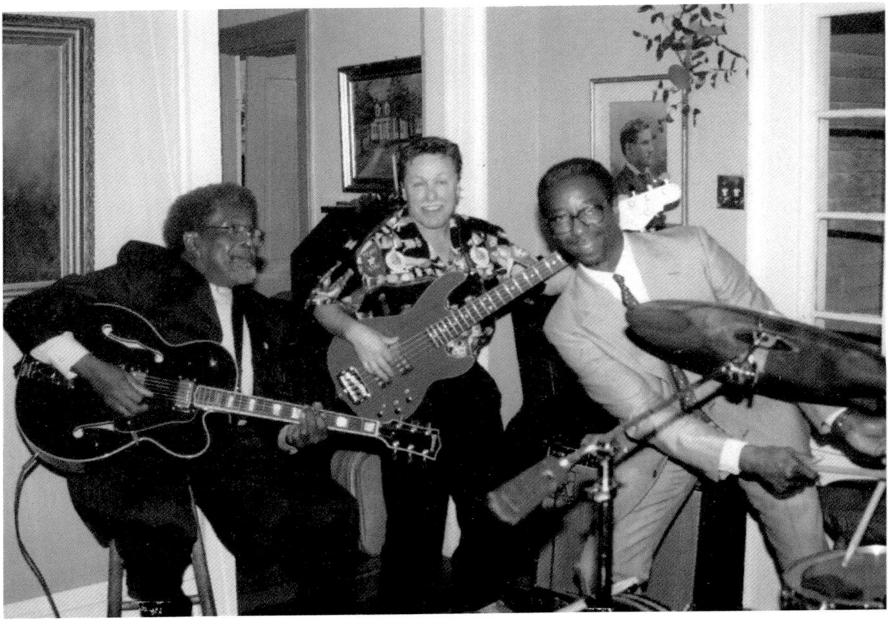

Drink and past sidemen. *Courtesy of Drink Small, personal collection.*

*"you playin' with all this here. That ain't how you play the blues. That's how you play what they call the folk blues."*

*"What the hell does that mean?" I asked, voice cracking with anger at what I took to be an insult.*

*"Well now, ya see you play the blues with this here," Drink stated, holding up his right thumb and index finger. "This gives you the strength to play some blues on this ol' guitah."*

*"Drink, I don't know what you're getting at," I protested. "But if you think you can play anything on that piece of junk, I'd like to see it!"*

*Drink chuckled to himself again, and then he laid into that guitar. I immediately recognized the ragtime changes that flowed effortlessly and perfectly from beneath his fingers. Drink's mouth was open, and he shouted out his version of the "Rag, Mama, Rag." Even as I write this, the hair on my arms is standing straight up as it did that day. This was the "real deal," I realized. Although I already knew it, Drink demonstrated that he had "the stuff." My jaw went slack and headed for the floor as Drink finished the tune. Grinning, Drink looked at me with a twinkle in his eyes. "That's the way you do it, boy."*

*I was speechless. Shoulders stooped and head bowed, I picked up my coat, mumbled a thank-you and headed for the door, shaking my head. I'd been "had" and got myself a good spankin' to boot. Behind me, I heard Drink begin a laugh. A chortle that eased into a loud guffaw. "Don't feel bad, boy," he enthused with a loud "hah, haw." "You keep workin' at it and come on back when you really know somethin'!" Speechless, I climbed into my car and headed south toward Charleston and home. I don't think I stopped shaking my head in disbelief at my own hubris and what I had witnessed until I pulled into my driveway.*

## *Oscar Rivers, Charleston, South Carolina*

Oscar Rivers Jr. is a well-known South Carolina jazz musician. In the 1950s, the Burke High School saxophone prodigy went to South Carolina State College to study music and meet jazz greats such as Skipp Pearson. On the weekends, Rivers would take the bus from State College to Columbia, where he would attend parties and gig with other talented musicians. Although he was only eighteen, he was an extremely gifted saxophone player, and he met Drink Small almost immediately. Drink was establishing himself as a blues musician at the time and needed high-quality artists to play local gigs with him.

Rivers was a serious musician who understood music theory and composition—a perfect match for Drink Small. In a personal phone interview, Rivers said, "I have a lot of respect for Mr. Drink Small, and I learned a great deal. He was serious about music, and he was also a fun-loving blues and boogie man. I remember we played all over South Carolina, riding in the car for hours eating pickled pig feet [laugh]. We did a really big party near Orangeburg. I don't how we got the gig, but when we got there, everyone spoke Spanish. I don't think anyone even knew what Drink was singing, and he just kept making up lyrics and adding a Spanish beat and they went crazy. All we could do was try and keep up!"

After graduating from South Carolina State College at the age of twenty-one, Rivers left South Carolina to go to Chicago. After he arrived in the Windy City, he met jazz great Sonny Stitt, who immediately invited him to join his band. "He was so impressed with my playing at the young, tender age of twenty-one," recalls Rivers. "I told him I'd just moved there from South Carolina. He was just up in arms." While in Chicago, Rivers played with the Quincy Jones Orchestra, Stevie Wonder, B.B. King, the Temptations and the Jackson Five.

Rivers remained in Chicago from 1961 to 1979. Despite working with the era's most successful musicians, it was a difficult time to make ends meet as a player. He was able to supplement his income by teaching music at Chicago-area schools. He returned to South Carolina, and one of the first calls he got to welcome him back home was from Drink Small: "the blues and boogie man called me up."

Rivers gigged in many bands on keyboards before he and his late wife, Fabian Rivers, formed Rivers and Company. Oscar has taught for decades in Charleston County public schools. He founded, leads and accompanies the Morris Brown AME Church Gospel Choir. His trademark on the alto is "April in Paris." He performed with the Charleston Jazz Initiative Legends Band in 2010 and is featured on its first CD recording. Oscar Rivers stated, "He's [Drink] a great man. No matter where you go, there's nobody like Mr. Drink Small."

## *J.T. Anderson, Bass Guitar, Columbia, South Carolina*

J.T. Anderson is a regular visitor in the Smalls' home. He is not so much as visitor as a longtime, close personal friend. J.T. is one of Drink's protégés, and as Drink's wife, Drina, said, "J.T. will come by and ask for Drink's advice. Drink has been knowing him for years. He's a really good guy."

J.T. is a South Carolina native who has played with countless blues and R&B bands in his home state. He joined Elliot and the Untouchables in 1997, a year after harmonica player Mike "Naz" Nazarenko joined the group. Nazarenko, who grew up in the Panama Canal Zone, had also played with Drink Small.

J.T. was adopted at the age of four by Fannie Mae Gorey, and she bought him his first guitar and even a trumpet. When J.T. was about thirteen, his mother purchased him his first bass guitar and amplifier. She was always very encouraging, and J.T. said, "I never made too much noise around the house as far as she was concerned." J.T. named his 1975 Fender jazz bass, which he used almost exclusively when he played with Drink Small, "Miss Linda." Like Drink, J.T. grew up in rural South Carolina listening to the blues late at night on WLAC-AM out of Nashville, Tennessee. Seeing a blues band play at a local juke joint struck a chord and inspired him to pick up the bass guitar. His mother provided him with a strong work ethic and respect for himself and others.

J.T. has played with countless gospel, blues and R&B bands in South Carolina for over a quarter century. His career in the U.S. Air Force allowed him to tour and play all over the United States and in England.

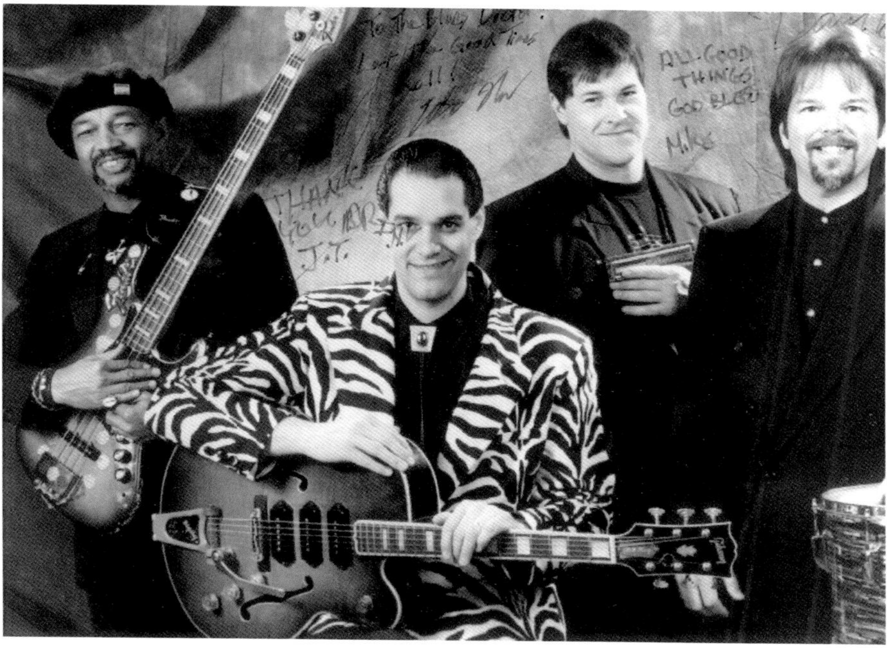

An early publicity photo of Elliott and the Untouchables band with J.T. Anderson (with guitar on left). *Courtesy of Drink Small, personal collection.*

J.T. says he learned a great deal from Drink Small, who mentored him for seven years. While with Drink, J.T. traveled to the New Orleans Jazz and Heritage Festival, New York City's Central Park and Lincoln Center. With influences from the juke joint to the church, from New Orleans to Chicago, from Motown to Trenchtown, J.T. feels the things he learned from Drink were how to engage the audience, how to bring feeling to everything you play and to always, always respect your craft. He said, "A bluesman has to look good—no showing up in tattered, unkempt clothes. Get yourself a pair of black paints and a nice shirt that you only wear on stage; it makes a difference." J.T. still has his guitar, "Miss Linda," and stated, "I look at it, at it's just like looking at a history book, because it has a lot to do with the time I traveled with Drink. That bass has been to New York, Canada, Florida. It's been to New Orleans, it's been all over." And at the heart of it all? "Feeling. I can't stress that enough. Feeling is what Drink Small is all about."

## *Elfi Lilliana Hacker, Winnsboro, South Carolina*

Elfi Hacker said:

> *The 145 Club is about music. Music is not a choice. It is a passion. Either you've got it or you don't. If you don't, that doesn't mean you don't appreciate or even love music—it's just that if you do have the passion, it will always be a common thread in your life. It will play a major part in the choices you make. I tend to think it runs in families.*
>
> *I was born in New York City* [Lenox Hill Hospital], *a first-generation American, in the early spring of 1955. My parents met in the late 1940s at the Liederkranz on East 86th Street, where my father (Austrian/Bohemian) was the first violinist in their symphony orchestra. My mother (German) was working and studying with a Juilliard professor, Weisa Ruben. Violin was not my father's profession; it was his passion. His profession (about which he was also quite passionate) afforded his family a cosmopolitan lifestyle that landed me back in Europe for the most part by the time I was fourteen, not before having experienced the Beatles invasion and the historic summer of music, 1968 in the USA—the music leaving a profound impact on my young, evolving self.*
>
> *If you have the passion, you will understand the gravitational pull—a magnet, always drawing you toward the music—making it, creating it, experiencing it. And so a lifetime of passion begins and grows. By the mid-1970s, I found myself in Munich enrolled at the university and a drama school. Quite unexpectedly, a local fashion designer asked me if I would model his collection, and thus my career as a fashion model was launched, which led to many more connections, countries and experiences. In 1978, I began a ten-year relationship with Egmont (Monti) Luftner (Ariola, Arista, BMG). Personally and professionally, these ten years were all about music—from angles and aspects I had not known or perceived. It was an education in all the wheels turning, all wanting to be greased, to profit from that spark of genius coming from one with the passion to make music.*
>
> *And me? I was the ears. And I listened with passion—to the music, to the makers of the music—because I could hear "it." I learned about the many lines that divide the industry—that "art" and "it" are not always the same; that "art" often does not translate into commercial success—the interests will always be divided. I did not judge. I listened. Life can change quickly. My father had a massive stroke and passed away in 1987. By 1988, with no other heir apparent, I assumed the day-to-day operations of*

*the scientific instrument company located twenty miles from New York City. This opened a chapter in my life. I got married; had an amazing daughter and son; developed, patented and launched a number of groundbreaking tissue-processing technologies and instruments. I got on with building the empire and maintaining the American dream.*

*Fortunately, there was an abundance of some of the best live music in and around Metro New York, so I could always recharge my batteries. In 2003, I woke up one morning knowing that I no longer wanted to live and raise my children where I was living. I set out to find a new home for me, my family and my business. By February, we had moved everything to Winnsboro, South Carolina. A major feat. Why Winnsboro ? There were all the logical reasons: better climate, lower population density, availability of land, interstate access, etc, etc.—conditions that can also be found elsewhere. The real reasons were things I could not put my finger on—a gut feeling. The 145 calling?*

*In practical terms, I knew nothing about the South. I had visions of Charleston, mint juleps and houses with white pillars—and most of all, great live blues music. The foundation of all the music I loved. I had this tourist's image of the blues pouring out of doorways…How naïve. That is no more—much like lederhosen are no more of Bavaria, except as a tourist attraction. And in those places where no tourists go, none of them would ever know…*

*There is a learning curve. We adjust. We adapt. South Carolina is good, but where is the music? Where is the blues? Mac's on Main, I'm told. Reverend Marv Ward is playing. Not a bad start.*

*New Year's Eve 2004, Winnsboro's Tavern (now sadly burned down) hosts live music with the Rev. I had talked the manager, Jimmy Russel, into getting Marv to come up and play. And Marv did an amazing job, for five hours, all on his own—a blues man. In January 2009, my mother passed away (age ninety-seven). This sad event allowed me to feel free to follow my passion and turn my family business over to my more willing and able ex-husband. Since moving to Winnsboro, I was involved with a number of community and downtown initiatives to bring the arts to Winnsboro and rejuvenate the downtown area. Resident artist Linda Dye owned and operated an art gallery on Congress (Main) Street and owned the adjacent building that had plans to become a coffee shop and photography studio. We orchestrated a number of live music events at various downtown storefronts, and I was constantly in Linda's ear about opening a club for live music. I guess I was consumed by my own vision. By August 2009, the Friends of*

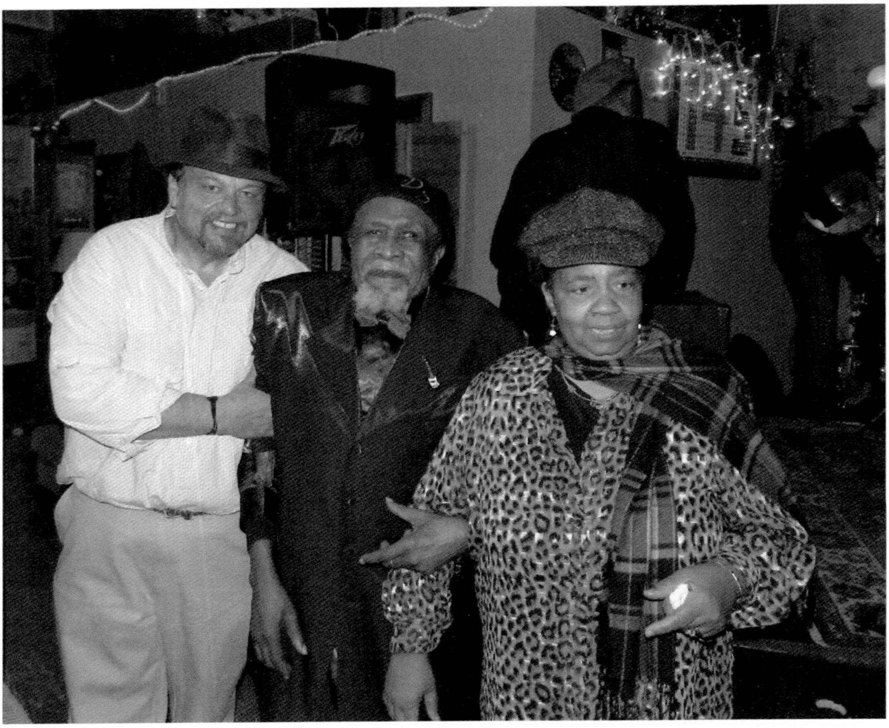

Jimmy Burroughs and Andrina escort Drink into the 145 Club in 2013. *Courtesy of Elfi Hacker.*

*Winnsboro's 145 Club was born—a private nonprofit club with a mission to support those creating and performing live music. The Friends acquired 145 South Congress Street to make it happen. Could it be a coincidence that 1-4-5 is the actual street address?*

*I did not have a large pool of musicians to draw from at the time—over the past few years, I had become aware of music that was being made locally—and once the doors opened on October 1, 2009, the music began to appear. And they played. Sure enough, one of my heart's desires was about to manifest itself. Jimmy Burroughs, a Winnsboro native and music lover, offered to introduce me to none other than the great Drink Small—the living legend, one of the true great-granddaddies of it all! Drink was a big part of my contemporaries growing up and coming of age in South Carolina. They had all heard him play live when he was young. YouTube, iTunes, iPhones and all those modern electronic miracles have come with a price...We can copy, document, re-create—but nothing beats the real thing!*

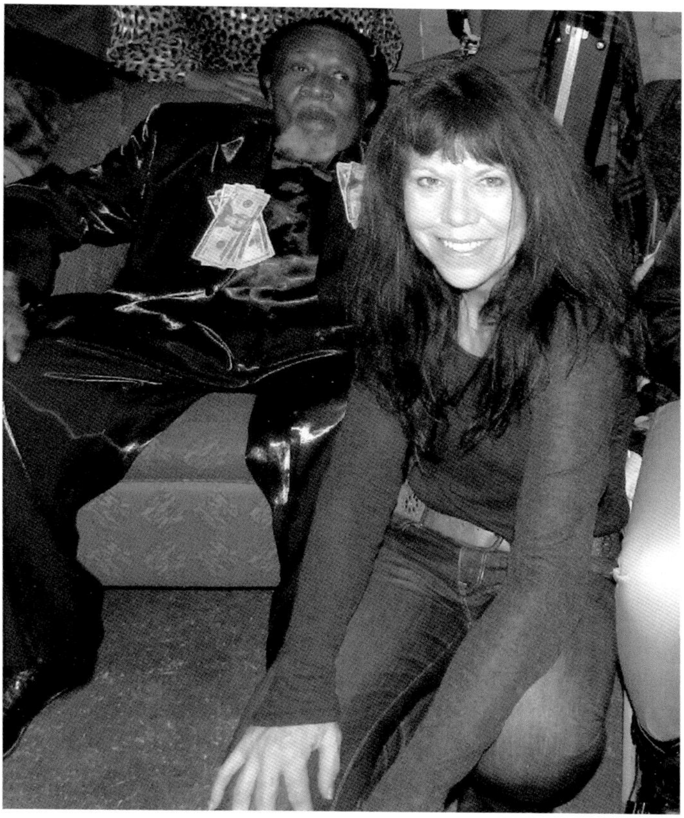

Drink's eighty-first birthday party at the 145 Club, Winnsboro, South Carolina. Drink is pictured with friend and club owner Elfi Hacker. *Courtesy of Elfi Hacker.*

*And so, for the first time in many years, the great Mr. Drink Small played live again in Winnsboro at the 145 Club on January 29, 2010. It was his seventy-seventh birthday celebration, and we have celebrated Drink's birthday at the club ever since. It is a rare privilege to be in the company of a living legend—one of the masters who set down the rules. To see and hear him do what he does and play the way he plays right there in front of you. What a unique window in time where practicing musicians can still sit down with and experience their own musical roots live—not just a recorded memory. The 145 Club is a journey about keeping the music alive so it can evolve and grow. There is an army of troubadours out there traveling the land, sharing their music, bringing beauty, joy and love to their listeners. It is a hard road for those who choose to practice this art, and it usually doesn't come with the conventional rewards and benefits. The 145 is home to all of these and all of those who enjoy listening to them.*

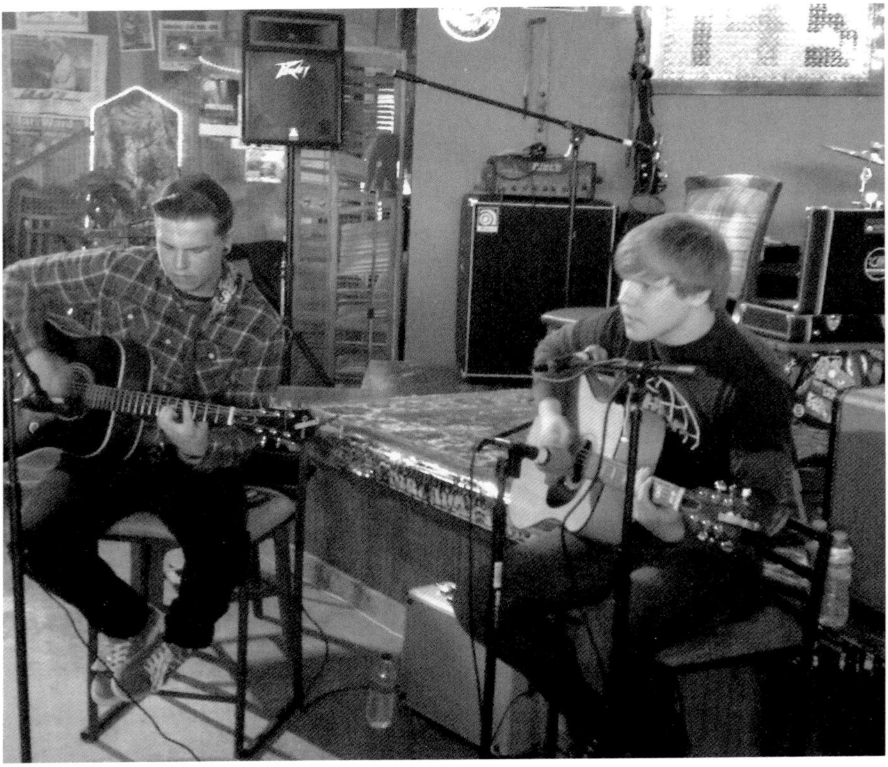

Martin Hacker Muller (son of Elfi Hacker) and Keagan McChesney of Oneforall perform at Drink's eighty-first birthday at the 145 Club. *Courtesy of Elfi Hacker.*

*Since our doors opened, our walls have been honored with some of our greatest living singers/songwriters, including Susan Gibson, Michael Hearne, Tish Hinojosa and Jimmy Davis. We have seen singers, songwriters and recording stars emerge from our community. Above all, we gather in peace to enjoy something greater than us, something that brings us all together and takes away our differences: the music.*

## *Chapter 4*

# LIVE AND OUTRAGEOUS

In 1990 and 1991, Drink recorded two albums, *Round Two* and *The Blues Doctor*, on the Atlanta-based Ichiban Records. Promoting the albums required touring and special guest appearances with the label's hottest performing artists. Curtis Mayfield was the headliner, and his success meant success of the label and therefore success for the whole Ichiban stable of artists. Drink was still being managed by Charles Derrick. For the big New York tour, they rode in one of Derrick's tour buses. Drink said:

> *I'll tell you what happened. It was a Monday night—I tell you what happened. That Sunday, we played at the Lincoln Center. I left there, and we drove up there to* [Rhinebeck, New York]*...me and Charles Derrick and Ben Sandmel; Ben was a drummer from Louisiana. Ben Sandmel, he's in charge of the music thing, and every time I played he's the one that got me to play at the New Orleans Jazz Festival. Only thing, you got to let him play drums, that ain't no problem. I done played there four times; in fact, I played there this year, and he played the drums...So we went up to Rhinebeck. So the school there was a vegetarian school, no meat, vegetarian school, no alcohol, no radio. I had just made my second album with the record company,* Round Two*...Derrick got a hotel room 'cause the school was no smoking, no alcohol, no meat...So that Monday after class, I went to stay at the hotel with Derrick. We had gotten something to drink. It was thundering and lightning, oh my God. So Derrick was going to the place where they have the ice. The lightning so bad, he started out three times. I*

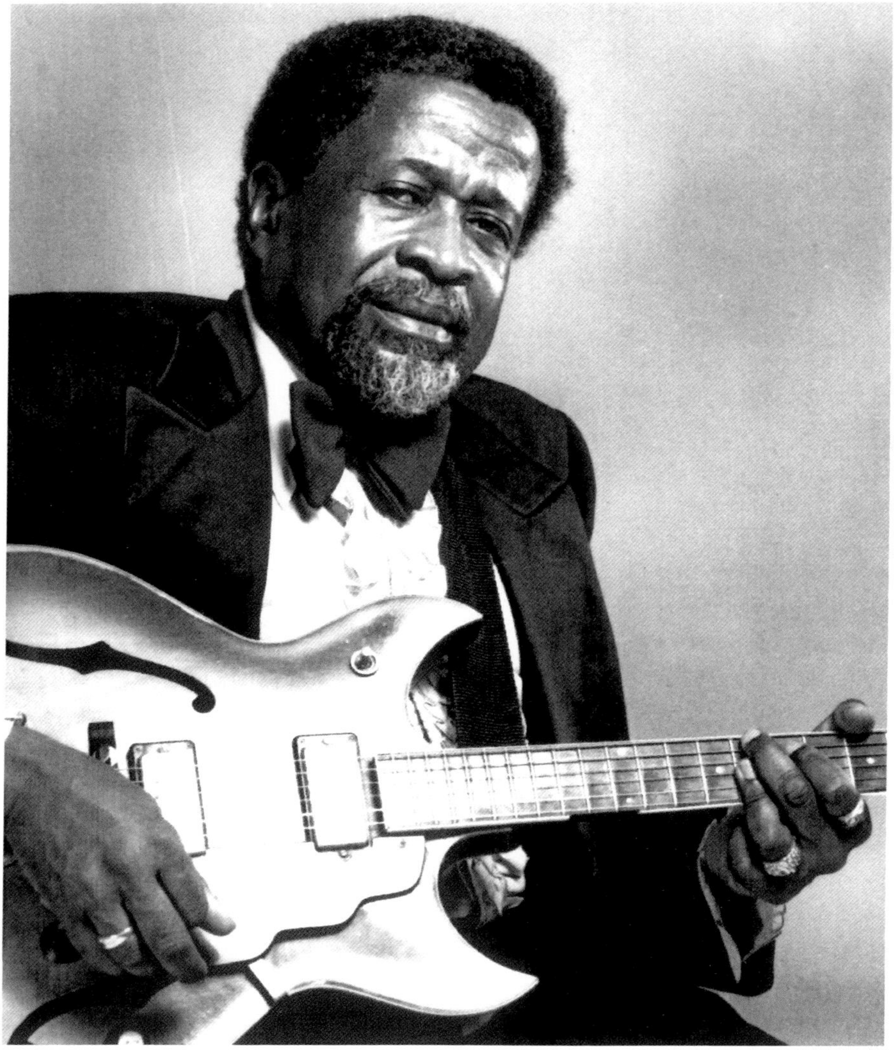

A 1991 Ichiban publicity photograph. *Courtesy of Drink Small, personal collection.*

*said, "Man, come on back in here." So we sit up in the room. The man on television said something about Curtis Mayfield. Three men standing there in suits, I can see 'em clear. All of a sudden something crashed and the picture started to dance, you know, started jangling, and they said, "Something—something's happened." They cut everything off. Later on,*

> *they said that a beam fell on Curtis Mayfield at the high school where he was playing in Brooklyn, New York. And the drummer say, "Look out, Curtis, look out." And Curtis went to get his guitar out the stand...and drummer say, "Look out!" That heavy beam dropped and fell down on him. Lord. And the next morning, the guy from the record company—I can't call his name, it's on the CD—flew up from Atlanta 'cause Curtis Mayfield was on Ichiban too; Curtis was one of the main artists.*

The tour was cut short, Drink returned to South Carolina and Ichiban suffered tremendous financial loss.

Charles Derrick knew that timing was everything. If Drink Small was going to capitalize on the Ichiban albums, he needed to go to Europe. African American blues and jazz musicians were being sought after by the European market. Charles Derrick had arranged a spot for Drink in the Finland Blues Festival. The problem was that Drink had a fear of flying. Drink was playing better than he ever had and was still looking for his one big break, so he decided to give it a try at least once. The entire time he was on the plane, Drink didn't get out of his seat; he was frozen and stared straight ahead. Once they got to the festival, Drink was sensational. He was the best musician there, and everybody went crazy for him. When the group returned to South Carolina, Charles Derrick received numerous phone invitations and letters all requesting live performances for Drink Small. Charles and Sam McCuen both tried desperately to convince Drink to do a European tour. Drink, however, stated he would never fly again. There are many people who truly believe that if Drink Small would have toured Europe and continued to do so once a year, he would most certainly be a millionaire today.

Drink really appreciates the fact that he has some following in Europe. Although he won't fly, he respects the way European audiences embrace and value African American blues musicians. He said, "They buy your music quicker than the one over here. It's new to them. We throw it away, it's new to them. You study classical music, music by Beethoven, Mozart, music that's five hundred years old. We call music fifty years old old; what about five hundred? Sometimes we American people are dumb...When we throw our history away." However, Drink continued to hold out and sustain his musical career in the United States and, in particular, at home in South Carolina.

In October 1991, Drink was one of seven traditional musicians from the Carolinas featured at the South Carolina State Fair. He opened for the Four Tops, exactly the type of work he loved. Unfortunately, his biological father,

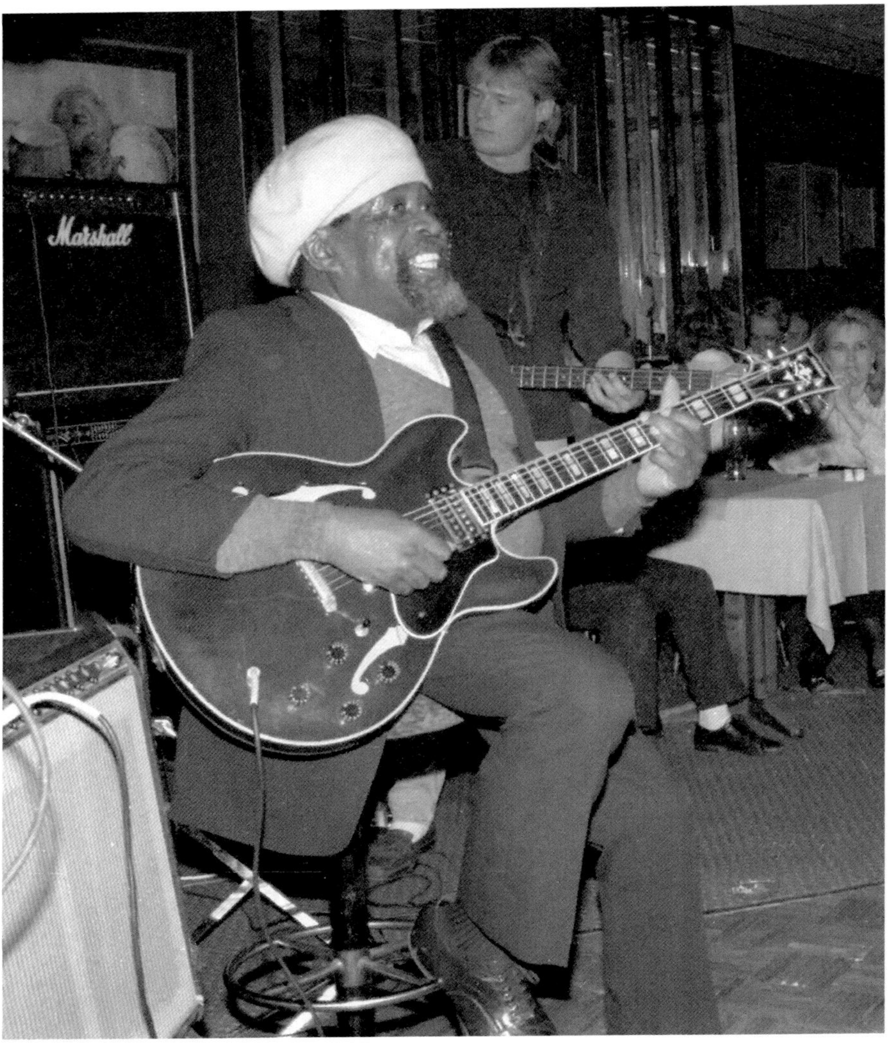

Arthur Jackson, died on March 27, 1992. He didn't have a relationship with him, but it was yet another personal loss. Drink did not attend the funeral and said, "He was living on Duke Avenue. I didn't know him, but he used to dance to my music in the clubs." Drink started making calls and writing songs and just stayed focused on finding work and making music.

In October 1992, Drink appeared two nights at the well-known Rosa's Lounge in Chicago. Rosa's Lounge maintains the tradition of Chicago blues lounges. It is still family owned and operated. The Italian immigrants came

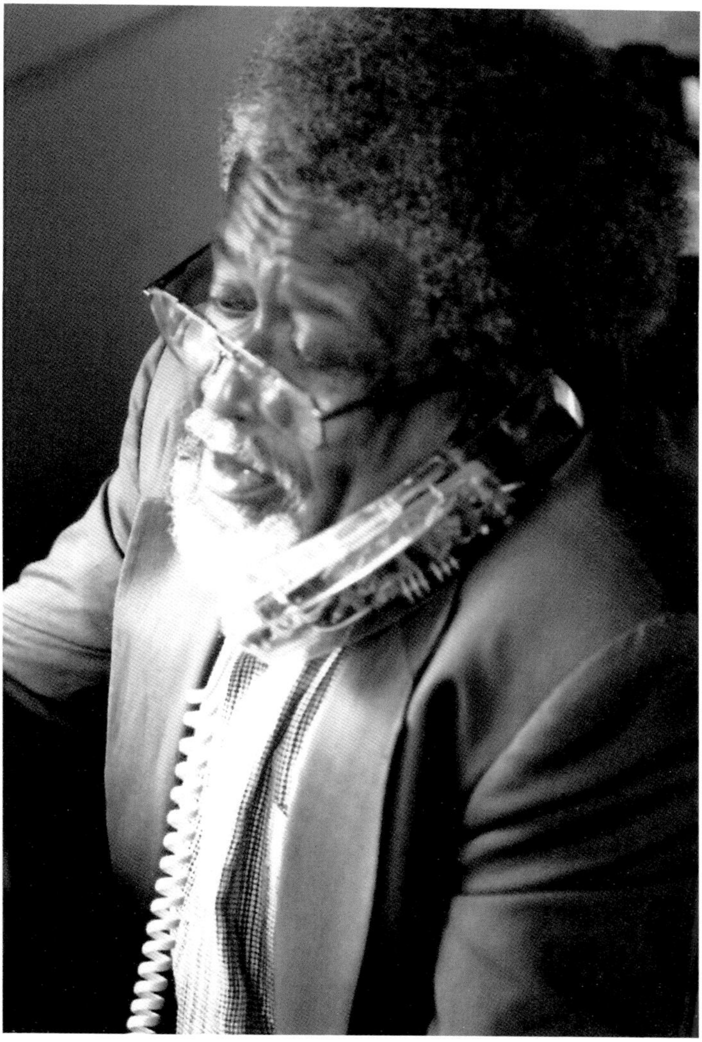

*Opposite*: Drink Small performing at the Kerava Jazz Festival, May 1991. *Courtesy of Pertti Nurmi-Blues Photography.*

*Left*: Drink on his see-through phone, 2000. *Courtesy of Cassie J. Fox (CazFox-Fowler) Photos.*

to Chicago in 1978 after meeting Junior Wells and Buddy Guy in Milan and were inspired to start the lounge. Drink had been performing in Charleston in the early '90s and was invited to perform at the club by a friend of the club owner. David Whiteis of the *Chicago Reader* described Drink Small as a "raconteur, songster, and showman—looks and sounds as if he just stepped off the stage of an old-time traveling medicine show. He bills himself as 'The Blues Doctor,' and his persona is a combination of avuncular warmth, carefully crafted musical expression, and flimflam (he boasts of using

14—count 'em!—different blues-guitar techniques in an eccentric stylistic gumbo he calls 'Drinkism')." Even with the colorful description, Whiteis also acknowledged Drink's talent: "Small is more than a quaint relic: he's a master at improvising lyrics in live performance, and his gifts as a storyteller are nearly as impressive as his musicianship. In turn ribald and poignant, irreverent and philosophical, Small creates a world of fantasy and delight, made all the more inviting by the ebullience of his personality."

He toured and continued to get bookings from his friends such as Gary Erwin and Charles Derrick. In 1993, they made trips to Toronto, Canada, and throughout the East Coast. Drink said, "That why I know so many people…I didn't keep no record; Derrick kept some. Made the headline of the *Washington Post*. I was playing a school in West Virginia, had a busload of classmates came over from Washington, made the front page. Man, I done been some places."

Drink had been around long enough and experienced enough in his life to understand that sometimes he was up, but much of the time he was down. The music plays on and on.

*I'm a crazy old guitar player*
*I got no sense and I telling everybody got the blues*
*Rich people got the blues but they trying to keep the money*
*Poor people got the blues got to try to get the money*
*I got blues but I got no money*
*Well the good Lord giveth and the good Lord taketh*
*Every day I got the blues*

Drink's reputation had attracted the attention of a young bluesman from Chicago and the education-focused program he had created. Blues in the Schools was a dynamic project led by Billy Branch and the members of his band, Sons of Blues, which they had been doing since 1992 in Chicago. The concept allowed students to spend time after school with professional blues musicians. After learning of the Chicago-based program, the idea was brought to Charleston, South Carolina, by Mary Feldman, a transplanted Chicago native and businesswoman. Feldman established the nonprofit Blues in the Schools Education Fund, and she and Billy Branch started collaborating to bring the program to Charleston and, soon after, to Columbia's middle schools. Billy met Drink Small through a Columbia school educator and quickly included the Blues Doctor in the program. The program was featured on Charles Kuralt's *CBS Sunday Morning* and NBC's *Today* show. Drink always enjoyed playing with the acclaimed Billy and

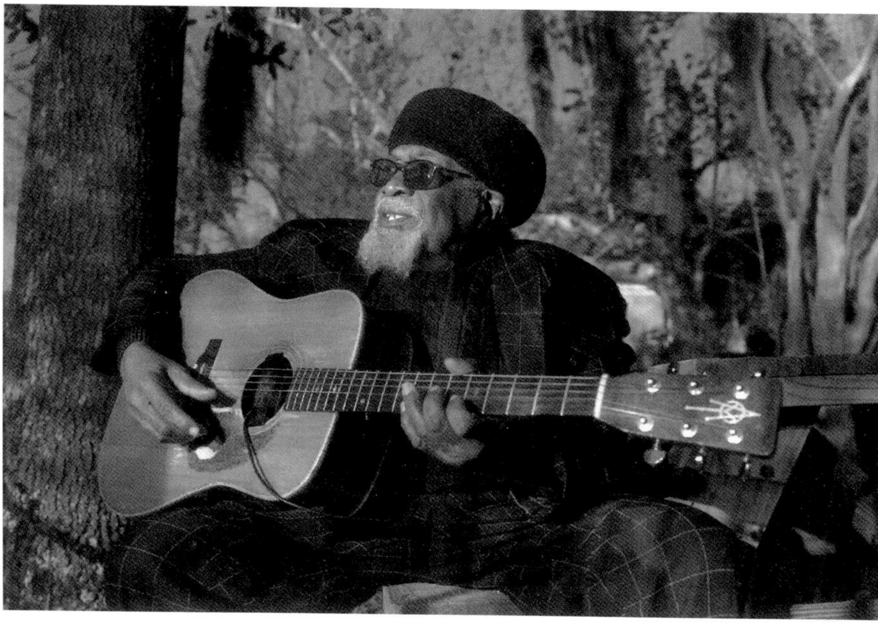

Drink Small and his guitar, Geraldine. *Courtesy of Drink Small, personal collection.*

appreciated the opportunity to share his talents and love for the blues with young people through this program, as well as through the New York–based Jazz Foundation of America. Drink was building a following of young fans in his home state; however, on a personal level, he was lonely.

In April 1995, forty-six-year-old Andrina "Drina" Bratton was working as a nurse and also helping out in the family diner, the Triple D, which stood for the names of the three sisters. She recalled, "We had a little small restaurant on Farrow Road, and boy did we have a lot of people. I opened up the restaurant in 1991, and I closed the restaurant in '98. Back in the day, everybody used to come—truck drivers, people from all over used to come and eat the food. They loved the food. Just a little small restaurant." The Triple D started out serving only breakfast. "I used to make the breakfast where we would have fish, grits with stewed tomatoes," she recalled.

The Triple D was so popular that it started serving lunch and dinner and hosting parties for the neighborhoods. It was especially popular with the local police officers. Andrina said: "Fish is a traditional black meal for African American people. Fish and grits, fish and rice…I had to move out from the restaurant and got me a wagon, and I fried fish right there on Farrow Road."

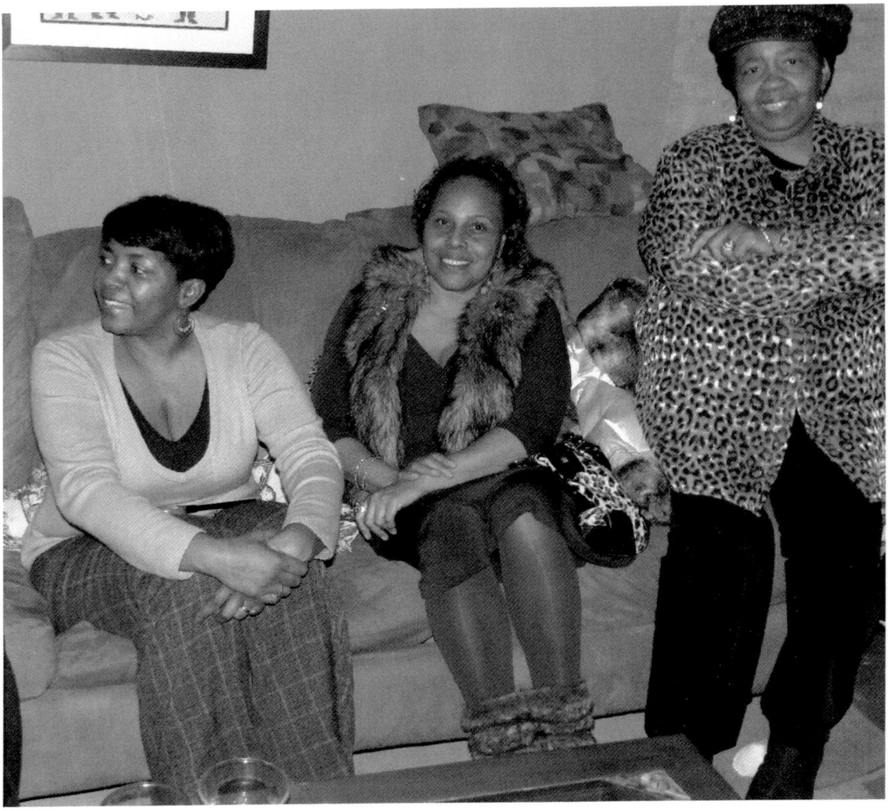

Andrina Bratton Small (right) with her sisters Renay Croft (left) and Doris Bratton (center) at Drink's eighty-first birthday at the 145 Club. *Courtesy of Elfi Hacker.*

She closed down the restaurant and purchased a food wagon with which she could travel around to festivals creating new ways to serve fish, including a fish dog: fish, coleslaw and mustard served in a hot dog bun. Andrina fried her fish with the popular recipe at city parks and expanded her offerings to other soul food like chitterlings. "Corn bread, macaroni and cheese, collard greens, my special rice and chitterlings. Those chitterlings were so good. I got the recipe from the older people. They said, 'Girl, you need to throw a chicken leg in there!' The chicken would give the chitterlings flavor—chitterlings, now, they got to be clean! That was what you call the soul food line, back in the day. I just loved that part of my life...and I'm still frying fish."

**Breakfast Special at the Triple D**
Fish, Grits and Stewed Tomatoes
Andrina Bratton Small

Clean it up and split the fish on both sides.
Make sure the fish is properly dried off, real good.
Use salt and pepper; I always add a secret ingredient to make the crispiness.
Don't use a lot of meal.
Make sure the meal is put on so it won't be fat and flaky.
You want to be able to taste the fish.
Mix the meal with paprika and cayenne; you can make your own little batter with that.
Everybody will love the fish!

Drina was planning a Family Day event for over five hundred people. She wanted to provide entertainment and was asking who might be a good choice for her event. Many of her regular customers suggested she get Drink Small, the Blues Doctor. She did not know Drink; however, she had heard of him and decided to gave him a call. When he answered the phone, she was immediately taken with his trademark deep voice. Drina recalled how she drove to the house on Lady Street, mentally preparing herself to meet the man behind that deep, sultry voice. She arrived at the address, got out of the car and walked up to the house. She saw a small-framed older gentleman sitting on the porch. Drina said, "This fellow looked so undernourished. I asked him, 'Sir, I'm looking for Drink Small?' He responded, 'Well, I'm Drink Small!'" He just didn't fit the image she had in her head, and laughing, she said, "I 'bout ran through two stoplights trying to get away!" Andrina feels that all the time on the road had taken a physical toll on him, noting, "He's a sweet person. He is so into his music, he forgot all about Drink."

Their first date was at a restaurant on Millwood Avenue called Rays. Drink had arranged for a private room in the back, and the table was set with candles and flowers. When they arrived at the restaurant and walked back to the room, Drina asked him, "Oh, this is pretty, wonder who this is for?" They talked and found out they had many things in common, and the time flew by. It was getting late, and Drina had to leave. Drink said to her, "Well, young lady, I'd like to see you again," and then he just kept calling her. Drina said, "He was a real gentleman—always wore a suit. And 'that voice.'"

Drink, on the other hand, remembers the story a little differently. He said that he had always been popular with the girls and likes to add, "I learned everything there is to know about women and love because I been loving women for sixty-five years—well, sixty years, because it took five to figure 'em out!"

As much as Drink enjoyed the company of women, it was uncommon for him to show up at a gig with a lady friend. Drina made herself valuable to Drink and the musicians very quickly. Drina began traveling with Drink and referred to herself as

> *Drink Small's personal cook back in the day. I would always bring our own food because you be somewhere and you might not like their cooking! When we used to travel a lot, I would always carry all the food he used to eat, like chocolate and sardines, he like all that good stuff! Getting back to that traveling, they didn't have a microwave in the hotel where we were staying, that was in Savannah. I always precooked the food and had it on ice. I had some aluminum foil, and I used the coffee container* [maker]. *We had grits and bacon already in foil* [laugh], *grits, cheese, bacon and Drink always liked sardines. I used that coffee urn! I cleaned it off real good, but people were knocking on the door saying, "Where that cooking coming from? Drina at it again!" And I don't go nowhere without my skillet 'cause I got to eat. They think I have clothes in the suitcase—but I have food* [laugh]. *The band members would never go hungry because I'm always gonna have me something!*

Drink gave Andrina the nickname of "Fish Frying Momma," and she quickly became an important member of his inner circle. Often, musicians would stop over to her house on Truman Street, where Drink would often entertain friends including Bill Pinkney, another South Carolina native and original member of the Drifters. In the clubs, Drina grew accustomed to showing up and having people ask, "Who are you?"

After the Triple D closed, Drina made some renovations to her home to accommodate Drink's love for entertaining and her love of cooking. The attached garage was finished and made into a room for music and dancing. Andrina had a window put into the adjoining wall to serve as a pass-through from the kitchen. She said, "I could be in the kitchen, and Drink and all his friends could jam out in the garage. It was great."

Drink appreciated having a companion, especially with his continuing health needs. Drina continued to accompany him on gigs and was always with him for his annual birthday bash, be it rain, shine or even snow. One of the biggest birthday celebrations was in January 1998, the year South

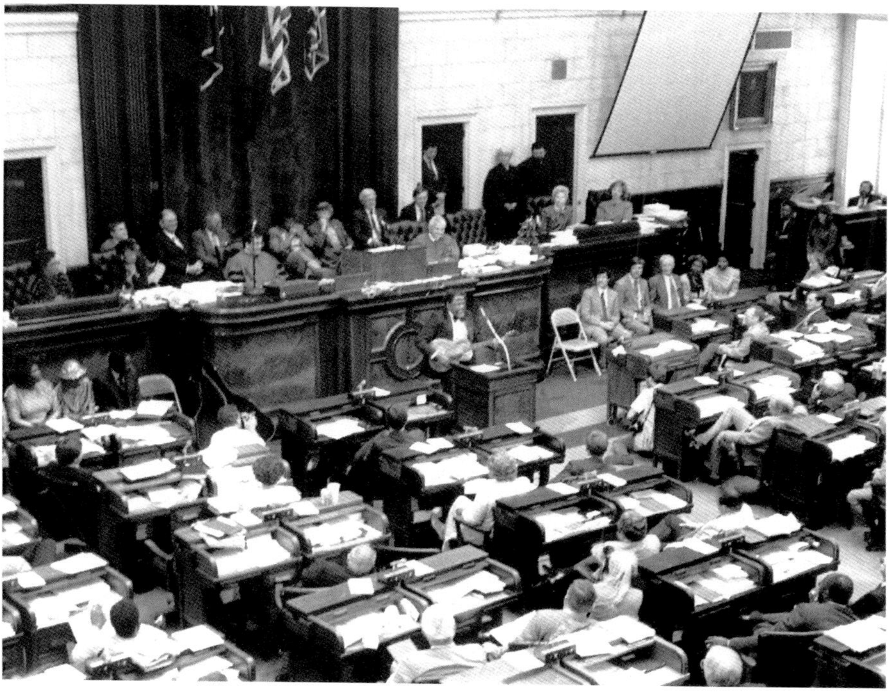

Drink being honored by the South Carolina General Assembly, Columbia, South Carolina, 1998. *Courtesy of Drink Small, personal collection.*

Carolina faced the extreme record-breaking weather patterns of El Niño. Drink recalls his sixty-fifth birthday: "1998, that the one where Mayor Coble was at, that was the corner of Washington and Main! Remember, Andrina, it got snowed out? They had to push it to the next weekend…It was two weeks to have it. Mayor Coble came; that when I got my first key to the city."

Despite the delayed birthday, it was one of those good years, and Drink was happy. The accolades and accomplishments continued right through 1999, when Drink was inducted into the South Carolina Music and Entertainment Hall of Fame, an honor he shares with such luminaries as James Brown, Dizzy Gillespie, Joanne Woodward and his friend Bill Pinkney. And once again, Drink received yet another key to the city. Drink laughed, saying, "I got two keys to the city, but what I need is a key to the bank!"

That same year, his old friend Nappy Brown was inducted into the Blues Hall of Fame. Drink was keenly aware of the grueling schedule his friend endured throughout mid- to late 2000. Gary Erwin would often feature

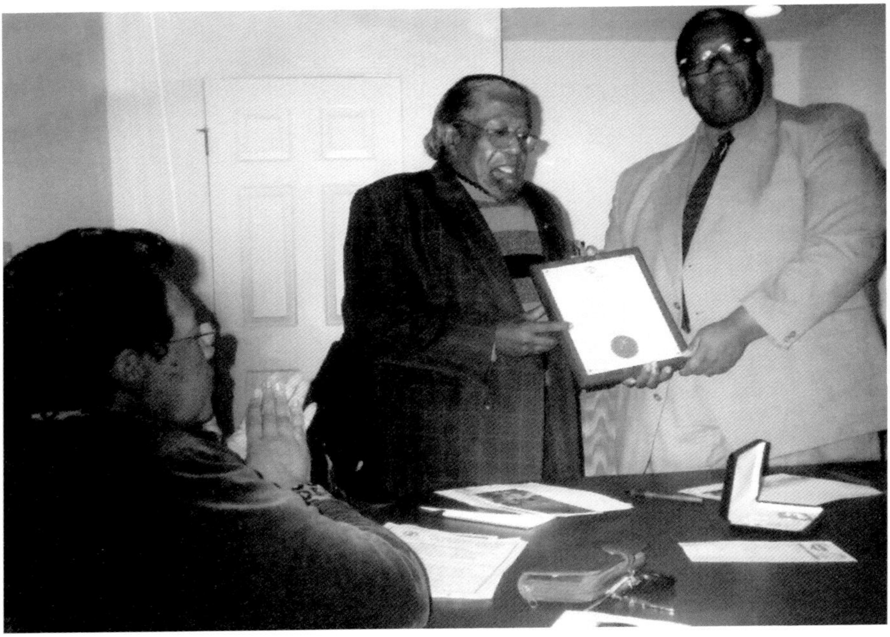

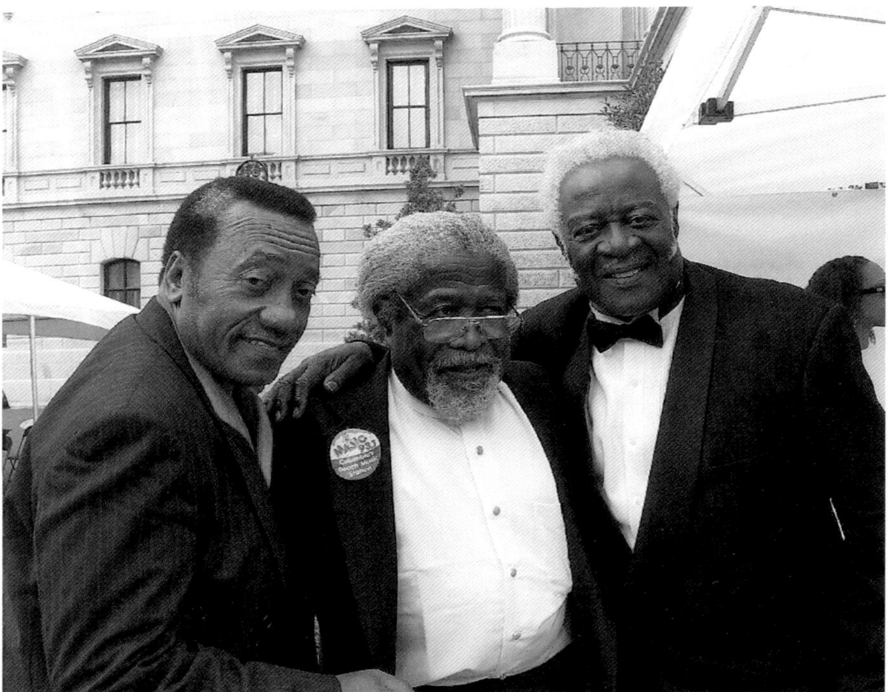

Drink and Nappy Brown at festivals such as the Festival of Discovery and Greenwood Blues and Barbeque event. Drink and Andrina both were concerned about Nappy Brown's health. Like all the other older bluesmen, Nappy Brown had to keep performing in order to pay the bills. There was simply nothing to fall back on.

Drink headed back into the studio and even established his own Bishopville label with the thought that this would provide him with a more economical way to record his music and distribute his own CDs. In 2002, he recorded *Drink Small Does It All*, which included original songs such as the song he wrote for Andrina, "Fish Fryin' Momma"; the humorous "You Don't Have to Funky," a country blues; and several spirituals such as "Motherless Child." On the CD, Drink included several songs dedicated to his beloved Palmetto State: "South Carolina Boogie," "Mr. Green Is the Barbeque Man" (written for Mr. Green, who owns several barbeque establishments) and "Living in a Barbeque World," the song written for the Greenwood festival. The CD was popular, yet none of the original songs were used in any major advertising campaigns, as Drink had hoped. However, that same year, Columbia mayor Bob Coble declared his beach music tribute "I'm Gonna Shag My Blues Away" as the official city of Columbia shag song.

All his life, Drink Small has been a magnet for blues lovers throughout the Palmetto State. With each passing decade, like the Pied Piper, he and his guitar, Geraldine, kept picking up new fans and friends at every turn in the road. Drink said, "You looking for pictures of me? Call Cassie; she's got some from way back."

Cassie J. "C.J." Fox (Cassie J. Fowler), a native of Whitmire, South Carolina, has been on the radio for the past twenty-four years. Cassie combined her professional and life experience with her love for blues music to work as an artist booking and management agent, concert and record promoter and public relations person. Cassie's clients included Drink Small; South Carolina's ambassador of jazz, Skipp Pearson; Maurice Williams and the Zodiacs; and Billy Scott, once known as Billy Scott and the Georgia Prophets.

*Opposite, top*: Drink receives a key to the city of Columbia, South Carolina, in 1998 from Mr. Odell Stuckey. *Courtesy of Drink Small, personal collection.*

*Opposite, bottom*: Drink Small (center) with Maurice Williams (left) of Maurice Williams and the Zodiacs and Bill Pinkney (right) of the original Drifters, Carolina Beach Music Award inductees. *Courtesy of Drink Small, personal collection.*

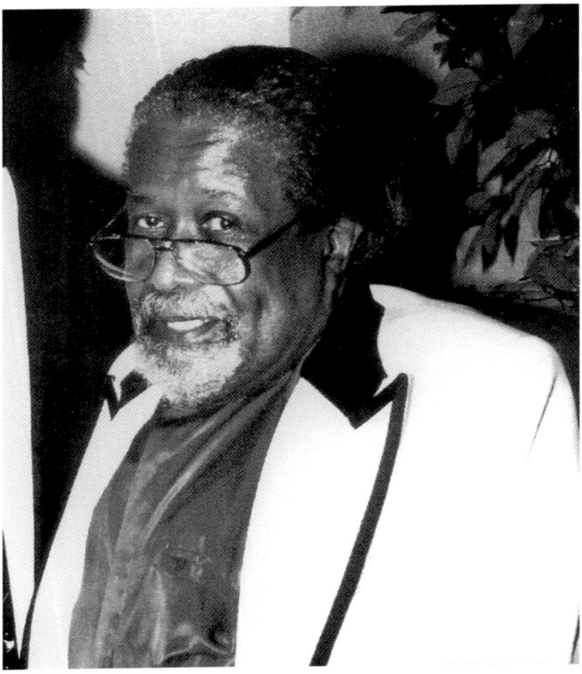

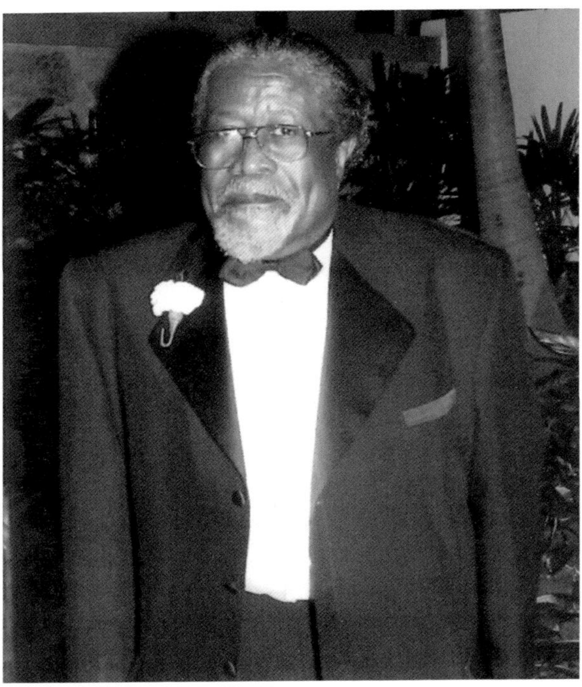

*Top*: Drink Small attending an award ceremony. *Courtesy of Drink Small, personal collection.*

*Left*: The 2002 South Carolina African American History Calendar Award celebration. *Courtesy of Drink Small, personal collection.*

Even as a child, Cassie loved and took an interest in music, specifically broadcasting. Her father and cousins owned Fowler & Lusk Skateland roller-skating rink in Newberry in the early to mid-'60s. The music was provided by a jukebox filled with Top 40 pop & R&B hits. Cassie was fascinated by the small public address system, the Green Hornet–shaped microphone, the older tube models and how the jukebox was restocked with new records on a regular basis. Her father, "Red," would come home with a stack of 45s from the jukebox for Cassie to play on the family Motorola console stereo. Her mother, Dorothy "Dot," not only taught Cassie and her brother Terrell how to skate but also used her S&H Green Stamps to buy Cassie a beginner microphone so she could "play disc jockey" and announce the songs and artists by plugging her mic into her small guitar amp. When Cassie was a young child traveling through the South, the family would stop at diners or restaurants, and Cassie remembers that most of them had jukeboxes. When the soul music would play, Cassie observed how the African American patrons and employees would immediately start humming or singing along. In the '60s to mid-'70s, her family vacationed on the South Carolina coast at her grandmother's house in Myrtle Beach. She always loved cruising with her family on the Grand Strand with the windows down and the radio tuned to WQZK-AM as they rode by outdoor tourist attractions. At that time, a drive on the Grand Strand toward North Myrtle Beach required passing through Atlantic Beach, the segregated beach designated for African Americans. The smell of home-cooked food, the pulsating rhythms from the jukebox and regional live bands and laughter and shouts drifting through the car windows from the small clubs and restaurants fascinated Cassie. She dreamed and fantasized about how when she was older, she was going to sneak into the dance clubs and halls to watch the show bands, listen to the jukeboxes and watch folks dance.

One thing to keep in mind is that at this time in history, there were not very many females spinning platters in clubs or hosting R&B/soul/rock-and-roll shows on the radio. Women in radio were relegated to hosting cooking shows or locally oriented community topics and programs. Cassie would stay up late with a single earpiece on a transistor or in the car to listen to WORD-AM Spartanburg; powerful nighttime frequencies like WLAC; WABC (Wolfman Jack); WOWO-AM, Fort Wayne, Indiana; WLS-AM, Chicago; and WWL out of New Orleans. The defining moment—"Oh yes, this is it for me"—for Cassie was when her fifth grade class performed for the Tri-Centennial Celebration in the studios at WKDK-AM in Newberry. That experience in the local station's studios left Cassie in awe of the entire scenario of her classmates singing into a boom mic and the announcer in the control booth playing music and station jingles. The small cities and towns of Union, Newberry and Whitmire produced several local and regional bands. Cassie would sneak down to the center and prop her bike up against the building so she could stand on the seat and gaze through the window to watch and listen as these groups rehearsed. The town's community center, known as the Canteen, was the social gathering place for the local Friday and Saturday teen and young adult dances. Groups included the Original Villagers (some of whose members also performed with the Greenwood County–based Swinging Medallions); the Whitmire-based Blue Majestic, with the only female keyboardist, vocalist and guitarist; and Martha Suber, who would go on in the mid-'80s to form one of the few all-girl blues groups, the Sensible Pumps (who opened for KoKo Taylor) and, later, the co-ed Mattie Phifer Band. The Whitmire-based R&B show band Johnny and the Magnificent Grooves featured Whitmire natives the Murphy brothers (Jesse and Delbert, aka Del) with their two sisters, Linda and Gail. Martha (known as "Mott"), Linda and Gail inspired Cassie. They were the few females in the area to perform rhythm and blues, soul and rock-and-roll in the male-dominated music scene. The roots and threads of these early experiences with Whitmire musicians would lead them all into a future blues mix with Drink Small in the coming years.

Cassie met Drink Small in 1999, when she was hosting a seventy-first birthday concert for South Carolina radio personality the late Cornell Blakely at the Newberry Opera House. Cassie and Drink became friends. Cassie helped him package and market his CDs, took high-quality press photographs and gave him rides to the store or to run errands. She stated, "He is such a thoughtful, good and kind man, a Christian man who took care of his son, Anthony, and mom, who was then confined to a wheelchair. He took her to doctor appointments, made sure bills were paid. When he had out-of-town gigs, he wanted whoever was driving to drive all night to get back home for his mother if she needed him." Drink was known for calling folks in the community on the phone and singing "Happy Birthday" to them. Drink and Drina Small gave Cassie her surprise fortieth birthday party, with live music from Drink and local musicians. Drink knew Cassie was still grieving over her mom's passing and was feeling down. The party was at Drina's, and Cassie said, "Andrina cooks that stick-to-your-ribs, down-home southern food that makes people feel good. We partied at her home in her converted screened-in carport, the room I called the 'speakeasy.'" Drink loved a big party so he could entertain folks with humorous "Drinkisms" and

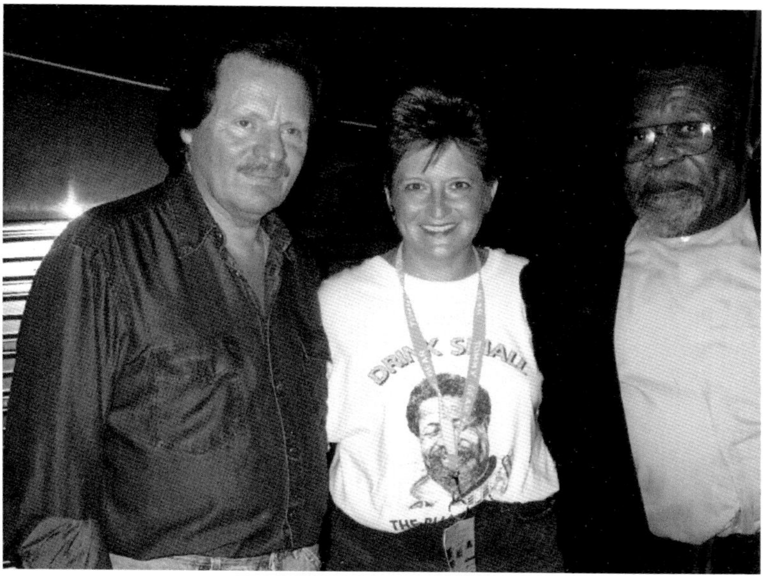



Drink with Delbert McClinton and Cassie J. Fox, 2000. *Courtesy of Drink Small, personal collection.*

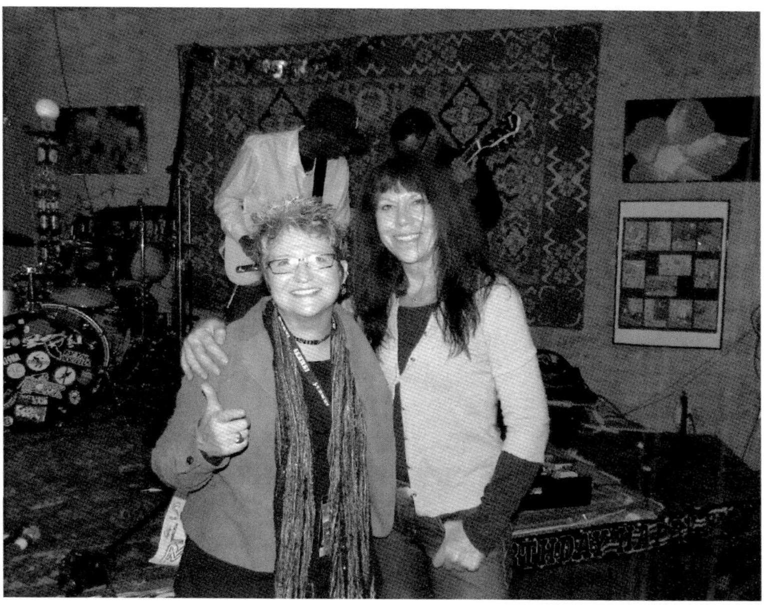

Cassie J. Fox (left) and Elfi Hacker at Drink's eighty-first birthday at the 145 Club. *Courtesy of Elfi Hacker.*

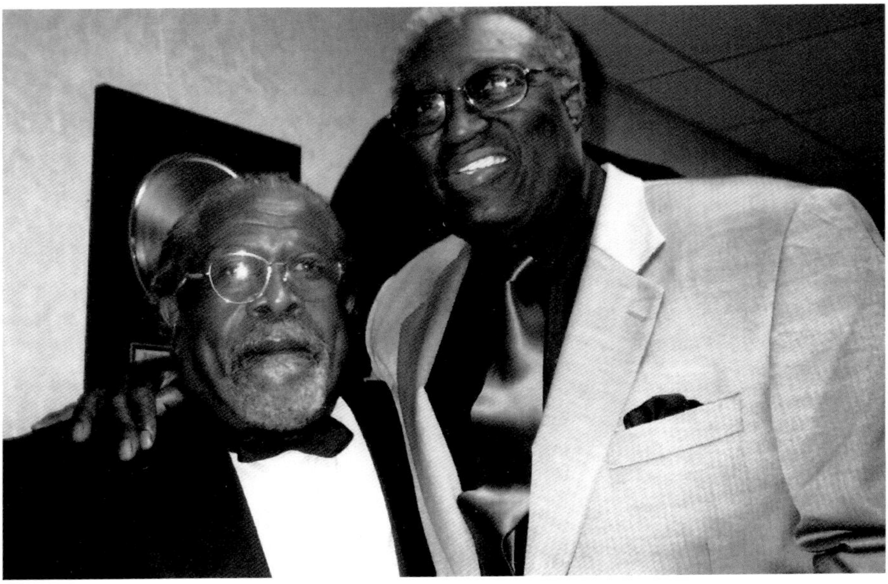

Drink with Harvey Fuqua (Motown and the Moonglows). *Courtesy of Cassie J. Fox (CazFox-Fowler) Photos.*

impromptu rhymes and songs. That particular party got pretty loud, with Drink and his musician friends jamming on electric instruments. A neighbor called the police, and the next thing the partygoers saw were the blue lights flashing from the local police. Drina, in her deadpan humor, responded without missing a beat, "Can you believe this? The neighbors calling the police to a black neighborhood for loud music!"

In 2001, Cassie, along with jazz-blues saxophonist and bandleader T.T. "Skipp" Pearson, coordinated Drink's sixty-eighth birthday party in Columbia's Vista area at the Blue Martini Listening Room. She said, "It was a huge event. Elected officials, television and media personalities, business executives and musicians packed the club to standing room only. The dance floor was crowded." Cassie remains a champion for the blues as the on-air host and producer of *Soul of the Blues with Cassie J. Fox*, her syndicated Internet radio show. She cares about Drink Small deeply and remains a dear friend of the family to this day.

Andrina was spending a great deal of time with Drink; however, she maintained her own house. In 2005, an electric fire in the dryer caused a house fire while Drina was at work. By the time she came home, the house had burned down, and she was only able to save a few personal items and pictures. What didn't burn was stolen. Drina bounced around to the homes of friends and relatives while her house was being restored. After the restoration, Drina was going to move back into her house, but Drink's vision was getting worse and he was experiencing other health issues concerning his breathing and even difficulty walking. Drina's experience as a nurse and professional care attendant were required. Andrina rented her house, Glenn Anthony moved in with his girlfriend and Drink and Andrina moved in together in the small brick house on Truman Street, where they continue to reside today.

Many of Drink's friends and acquaintances had grown accustomed to interacting with him on their terms. Now they had Andrina to contend with, and for some, that could be a problem. Drina believes her keen ability to detect a person's motive has helped protect them both. If you are honest and good, you won't find a sweeter woman, but if you are trying to take advantage of or be disrespectful to Drink or anyone in her inner circle, watch out! When it comes to Drina's more protective nature, Drink said, "I warn 'em. You better run!"

At the nightclubs, Drina would sit over to the side and watch the crowd, observe people to make sure nobody was trying to try cheat Drink. Drina appreciates Drink's sense of humor, stage persona, tongue-in-cheek jokes and flirtatious nature. Drink said, "I'm not only a blues player who teaches people about the blues; I also teach people how to make love. Before I make love to a woman, I take her down to the thicket and listen to Wilson Pickett." During many late-night performances, Drina said it was not uncommon by the end of night of music and dancing for some woman to sit on Drink's lap. Drina said. "Oh, they just laughing and giggling. They would even put their phone number in his pocket. I'd be the first one to tell him, 'You go on, Drink Small, might as well have yourself a good time.'" At home, Drina would come across the phone number and give the enthusiastic fan a call: "Hey, you wanted Drink to give you a call? So what is it you got to say?" Drina believes that it just takes up too much time being jealous. After all, most of those women are longtime fans and friends because "everybody loves Drink," she says with a smile.

Andrina arranged a gig for Drink herself. While working as a rehabilitation aide and staff nurse, she helped coordinate a series of performances at the South Carolina Vocational Rehabilitation Evaluation Center. Drink entertained patients in the cafeteria. Drina said, "One gentleman had been a guitar player, but he had an accident, left him with a brain injury, and he said he couldn't play anymore. Drink told him to play along anyway, and he did! He played for those people like it was a big-time show—and everyone just loved him. He did all his songs and wrote a new one on the spot, called it 'Wheelchair Boogie.'" Andrina has tremendous respect for Drink's musical and intellectual abilities: "He is a very smart person and knows a lot about black history. I just can't understand why one of those colleges don't promote him. The man has an elephant head!" Drink loves and respects Andrina and has written two songs about her, "Fish Fryin' Momma" and "The Nurse Song." He is fond of saying, "Only three things get me through this life: my God, my music and my wife."

Gary Erwin stated, "I got Drink on the Chicago Blues Fest in 2007, at the same time my band backed Wanda Johnson—a kind of South Carolina package on that year's festival. Drink returned several times on his own after that." In April of that year, the Southern Arts Federation held its "Folklorist in the South" retreat and twentieth anniversary celebration. The culminating event was a performance by Drink Small, "legendary Piedmont blues artist." This was indeed another great honor; however, the roller coaster of professional ups and downs continued. Five months later, Drink's friend Kip Anderson passed away in Anderson County, South Carolina, at the age of sixty-nine. On June 1, 2008, after a performance at the Crawfish Festival in New Jersey, Nappy Brown collapsed and was hospitalized. While visiting his old friend in the hospital, Drink was in the room at the same time as one of the musician's producers. Drink said, "He was holding Nappy Brown's hand and crying. He kept saying, 'I'm sorry, I'm really sorry. But I think we probably owe you money from those records you made.'" Nappy Brown died in his sleep on September 20 at Mercy Hospital. Drink traveled to Charlotte, North Carolina, with his wife, Andrina; Sam McCuen; and Clair DeLune. Drink was seated in the front during the funeral services, and at a separate memorial service for Nappy Brown at the Newberry Opera House in South Carolina, he was able to sing a song in honor of his dear friend and fellow musician.

The years seemed to be flying by. The devoted college student fans now had careers, children and even grandchildren of their own. Occasionally they might see Drink playing a local festival or event, and it always brought up deeply personal memories of youth and coming of age in South Carolina. It seemed appropriate that South Carolina Educational Television (SCETV) aired a segment on the history of the state's most popular nightspots. The program, part of the "Carolina Stories" series, was appropriately named "From the Famed Chitlin' Circuit to Tobacco Roads to the Bluegrass

Kerosene Circuit." The program's goal was to showcase artists who had made significant contributions to the musical landscape of South Carolina. Drink was the featured blues master, with other artists representing various genres, such as Bill Wells, noted bluegrass player and late owner of Bill's Pickin' Parlor in West Columbia.

Anytime Drink was acknowledged by his home state, he felt a tremendous sense of pride. The SCETV segment was popular, and Drink was honored to be featured with Bill Wells, a talented musician and a friend. Lousie Wells, Bill's widow, recalls that in the '80s, Drink would come to the Pickin' Parlor. He would sit in the front room of the music store, where a large circle of chairs was arranged for the banjo, fiddle, guitar and mandolin players who came on a regular basis. Bill's son Willie Wells tried to bring a monthly blues night to the Pickin' Parlor with help from Clair DeLune, host of the popular *Blues Moon Radio* and another compassionate friend of Drink's and all-around "blues goddess"; Gary Erwin; and a host of local and regional blues bands. Unfortunately, the blues night did not have enough local support, and far too often the large music hall would hold fewer than a dozen people. The bluegrass community didn't seem to embrace the blues, especially the louder electrified blues bands. And the blues community did not seem to fit in the tight-knight community of talented acoustic pickers and players that filled the music hall on bluegrass nights. So after a year of serious effort, Bill's Pickin' Parlor discontinued blues night. This was a real loss for the Midlands region. However, his respect and admiration for Bill Wells is something Drink speaks of often: "A nice man, a real nice man and a real good, I mean real good, guitar player!" Andrina added, "He was a good-looking guy, too, in his beautiful hat! We sure liked him a lot." Bill's signature hat is on permanent display on the stage in the music hall located in the back of the store.

Drink has respect for a lot of talented musicians, regardless of genre, and said, "Louis Armstrong was a game changer like no one else. He changed the direction of music. He was accepted by whites and blacks when he brought his big bands on tour…Now you take Sonny Boy Williamson—his harmonica is like speaking. He *is* talking, talking baby…And look at B.B. King—he works hard. That man must work 350 days a year. A real blues man is a blues man forever." Country, American roots and blues—Drink has loved and learned from it all.

South Carolinians interested in the state's traditional cultures, partnered with the South Carolina State Museum and the University of South Carolina McKissick Museum's Folklife Program to host a daylong conference. The conference included live performances throughout the day from musicians

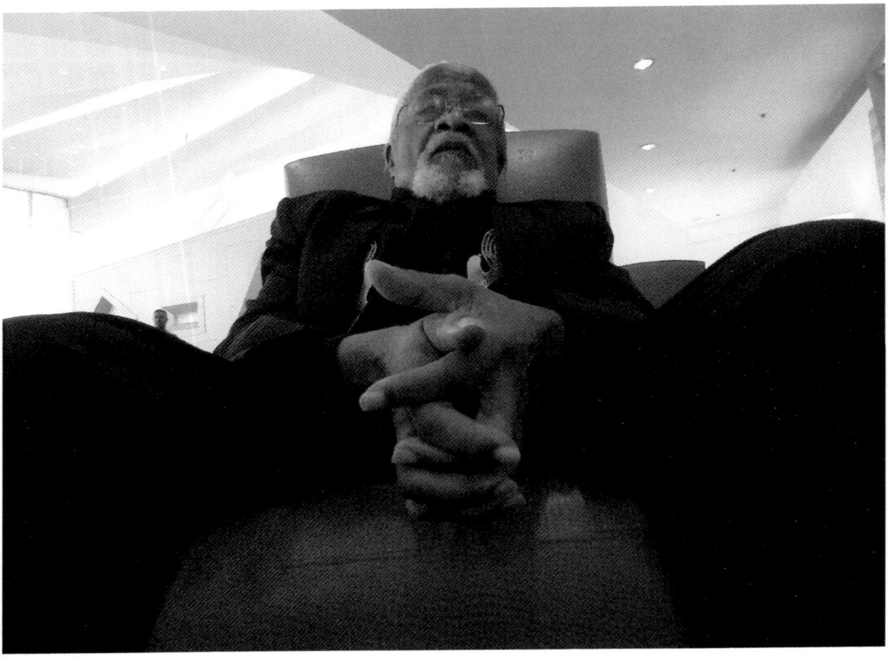

Drink seated in the lobby at the Memphis Hilton hotel for the 2013 Jus' Blues Music Foundation award ceremony. *Courtesy of Elfi Hacker.*

such as Maxie Branch Boys, Bill Wells and the Blue Ridge Mountain Grass and Drink Small.

Drink had another opportunity for commercial success with the song "Drink Don't Drive." He recalled, "Sam [McCuen] had a relationship with the transportation man, so my song 'Drink Don't Drive,' Sam had that played by the highway department. Me and Sam went to Greenville, Columbia back down to Charleston, and they used to play that song. I played it again, and they had something they called, 'Highways are die-ways.' I went up there, they had me playing at the state transportation place. Me—Drink, please don't drive…If I call that man, the man down there with transportation, he knows me. I betcha I can get that song played again 'cause so many people wrecking. And I wrote the song, and they played it on the radio here."

In 2010, the Historic Society of Bamberg County held the first Julius Daniels Memorial Blues Festival at the Dane Theater in Denmark, South Carolina. The event was established to honor the native Piedmont bluesman. Drink Small was one of the festival's first performers. It turned out to be an important event, as Drink received an honorary doctorate degree from Denmark Technical College.

Drink enjoyed sharing the news of this honor with his friends and family. Of course, Drink loves talking to his friends, especially his musician friends. His door was open, and he welcomed phone calls, saying, "I had the same number ever since I come to Columbia. I'm easy to find." Shortly after receiving the degree, he received a call from Chicago; his friend Billy Branch was going to be in South Carolina performing and wanted to get together. Drink had not seen Billy since the Blues in the Schools programs, and Billy had a fondness and respect for the older musician. He was looking forward to spending some time with him; it would be a nice reunion. Being from the city, Billy also appreciated the natural beauty of South Carolina; however, there were things that he continued to find challenging. By this time, Billy was really making a name for himself. He was a Grammy nominee and an Emmy Award winner, and his band, Sons of the Blues, toured internationally on a regular basis. He had just arrived in South Carolina when he had an unfortunate exchange with the owner of a local business. The woman was complaining, and the next thing the Chicago bluesman knew, she blurted out something along the lines of, "I don't know why you niggers…" The woman immediately realized what she had said and quickly apologized. Billy let it go as well; however, he always marveled at what he imagined must be Drink's extremely high tolerance for the racial prejudice he must have experienced throughout the course of his life.

On the other hand, blues music in South Carolina seems to be a sort of equalizer, attracting a diverse group of people. The high-quality new festivals and venues bring together people from all walks of life. While staying at the historic Chesnut Cottage on Hampton Street, Billy and his band put on a blues performance in the intimate venue. It was a curious setting, with a diverse group of blues lovers crowded in the front parlor of the historic cottage filled with Civil War artifacts and relics. Drink was thrilled to play his guitar with his friend, the master harmonica player.

The next afternoon, Andrina spent four hours cooking and cleaning. She invited Billy, the band members and a few close friends to a fish fry and jam in the backyard of their house on Truman Street. Jimmy Burroughs from Winnsboro was among the guests for that memorable afternoon. The band was happy and grateful for the opportunity to kick back, relax and enjoy real soul food. Drina was in rare form; she hadn't cooked like that since her days operating her Fish Fryin' Momma food wagon. As Drink sat back playing his guitar and singing, Jimmy Burroughs recalls how Billy Branch leaned over

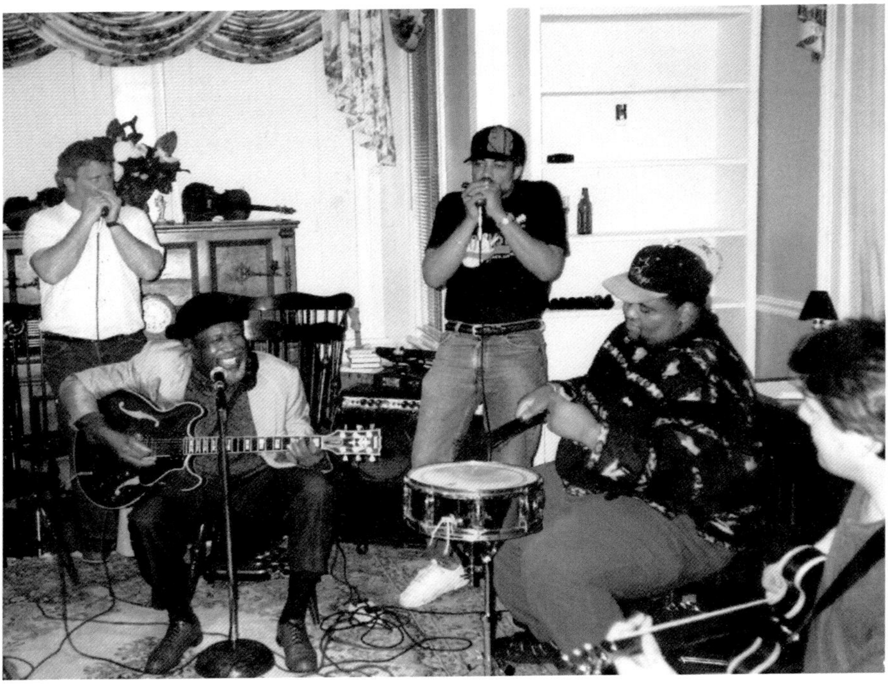

to him, pointed to Drink and whispered, "Take care of that man over there. He's one of the last of the true great bluesmen in the country."

The country might not have been celebrating Drink, but every January, you could still find someone in South Carolina very happy to do so. Gary Erwin hosted the seventy-eighth birthday celebration for Drink at the Bishopville Opera House. Carrie Gass, Drink's longtime friend from Dennis High School, and other childhood friends and family members all came out to help him celebrate. The local paper did an article, and Gary was quoted as saying, "For many in this part of the country, Drink Small is their number one blues point-of-reference." Gary continued to feature Drink at his statewide blues festivals, allowing Drink to connect with his fans throughout the state. As a result, one festival got its theme song. The Festival of Discovery boasted a weekend of blues music and barbeque vendors who competed for trophies and prices. The food vendors filled the street, and the blues musicians, booked by Gary, played in restaurants, galleries and stores throughout the picturesque town.

Drink composed the song "Living in a Barbeque World," and Gary submitted the tune to Uptown Greenwood Development Corporation,

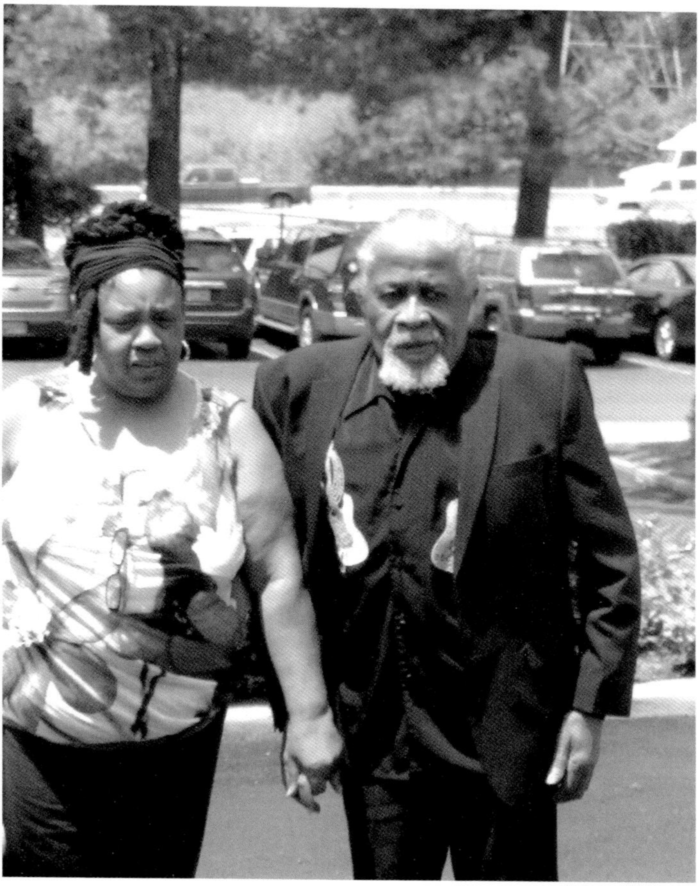

*Opposite*: Drink plays with Billy Branch at the historic Chesnut Cottage B&B. *Courtesy of Drink Small, personal collection.*

*Left*: Drink and Andrina Small, Memphis, Tennessee, 2013. *Courtesy of Elfi Hacker.*

which puts on the event in July each year. In the newspaper article, Gary stated, "Drink wrote it and put it out. He put it out after the Festival of Discovery, and it's just an obvious fit. He wasn't writing it for the Festival of Discovery. He was writing it for his passion for barbecue… 'The Blues Doctor' actually came up with an anthem for barbecue. It couldn't be more fitting and apropos." The song was enthusiastically embraced by festival officials because it celebrates not only barbeque but also South Carolina.

Drink has always incorporated gospel, beach, jazz, country and bluegrass in a style he calls "cross-up Piedmont." Cross-up Piedmont not only describes his music, but it also seems to describe Drink Small himself—a South Carolina original.

Drink enjoys spending time with Andrina's extended family, especially the grandchildren. The children all love Drink very much and would help him find items, look for his shoes, get the phone and simply keep "Big Daddy" company. In the spring of 2012, Drink and Drina were at home when Joseph, Andrina's four-year-old grandson, said to Drink, "Big Daddy, you should marry Grandma." The child then took a string and began to tie their fingers together. Drina said, "Drink looked at me and said, 'Well, I guess we should get married then.'" That is how they officially became engaged. It was a beautiful moment, stolen away too quickly. A few months later, Glenn Anthony Miller passed away as a result of cancer. Drink said, "Cancer, like blindness, is hereditary." However, that did little to console Drink: "Only son I got…You lose your only son, June 29. I'm 'bout totally blind, can't figure it right, feel like I wanna cry."

Whatever optimism Drink had regained was lost. He once again sunk into despair. The funeral was held on June 3, 2012, three days before what would have been Glenn's fiftieth birthday. Three months later, Drink and Andrina were married. The wedding was a simple backyard ceremony on September 30. Drink found it hard to really celebrate. He and Andrina were surrounded by a few family members and close friends. The ceremony was performed by a dear friend and minister who also had a beautiful voice, and Andrina watched as Drink and the pastor spent most of the afternoon sitting at the far end of the yard talking together. The pastor had been one of the original members of the Spiritualaires.

# PART II

# I'M TIRED NOW

*Chapter 5*

# ROUND TWO

During the late spring of 2013, Drink was not interested in being interviewed. He seemed preoccupied with death and dying. "This ain't the time to talk about the blues. This is the time to talk to Jesus. Pray with me; right now we gotta pray," he said. One moment he seemed to be grieving the fact that he was not a commercial success, and the next moment, he was denouncing material wealth: "See, some people that got money, they ain't got no soul, they ain't got no Jesus, they ain't got no mercy. Like a mule way back in the country, black man die—hire another one. Mule die, buy another. They ain't got no mercy." He was convinced that he didn't have long to live. "No, don't come to my house. This is a house for dying people," he told me on several occasions.

Drink caught a very serious cold, which he attributed to the senior center he had visited for services a couple of times. He didn't like leaving the house and didn't enjoy socializing with the other participants. His coughing had affected his voice, and he could barely speak, let alone sing. For the fourth time, he had been invited to participate in the prestigious New Orleans Jazz Festival on May 2, 2013, but this time he wasn't confident about making the trip. The long trip was difficult, and his inability to sing well because of his cold only depressed him further. "When I don't play up to my game, that when, Lord, I feel ashamed," he explained.

Consistently, he spoke about the need to find a different way to continue his career. After all, hadn't he done enough? He was tired now, and there seemed to be new blues musicians hired for the jobs he once had. "See, my thing is, I have made enough of a name. I need to get on the consultant part, not going out there performing, and let my prestige and experience speak for me…Matter of fact, they done run the blues in the ground. Everybody plays the blues now; it become monotonous. Too many people playing the blues, and some of 'em can't play. The blues not a regular, ah, ah, first-class music by society…The older ones 'bout gone now; only a few of 'em now."

The weeks following the New Orleans trip were challenging, but Drink got some wonderful news. He had been selected to receive the Bobby Bland Ambassador to the Blues Award from the Jus' Blues Foundation. The ceremony, scheduled for August 1, 2013, was to be held in Memphis, Tennessee. For Drink, the most exciting part of the honor was that the award would be presented to him by Bobby "Blue" Bland himself. To accept an award from a colleague of such note gave Drink a deep feeling of accomplishment.

While preparing for the Memphis event, he was struggling with a mounting variety of health issues. His vision problems just made everything worse. Drina was trying to coordinate with the Council for the Blind. Small had several appointments with his eye doctor, but he hated to leave the house. He said, "Every time I go, they put the drops in my eyes, and it gets worse. You go in thinking things gonna brighten up; it never does."

Drina had arranged for Drink to go to a senior self-care program a few days a week to learn skills to help him maneuver around more independently with his diminishing eyesight. He was taught to use a collapsible white cane, and a special mechanism was to be installed in their home for security. Drink did not enjoy the outings to the senior center. He said, "What am I going to talk to them people about? They don't know nothing about music. They should have an old folks' home for musicians. I'm an ole coon, and people don't have time for me. My poor wife gotta work; she come home so late she can't be taking care of me. I know why people commit suicide—no money, you sick, you blind. It's too much, too much."

This was a difficult time of year for Drink, for it was the anniversary of the death of his mother and his son. On June 23, Drink heard the terrible news that Bobby "Blue" Bland had passed away at the age of eighty-three, one month before the Jus' Blues Festival. Drink took the passing of his friend extremely hard. "Bobby Blue Bland died. Now he's gone, there ain't none of us left. I can't talk no more. I'm tired. I'm too tired to go on."

With his physical energy down and mounting medical problems, Drink said, "You don't understand. I'm a sick man. I thought I was tired years ago. I said, 'If it don't work this time, I'm gonna sit on my behind' [lyric from the

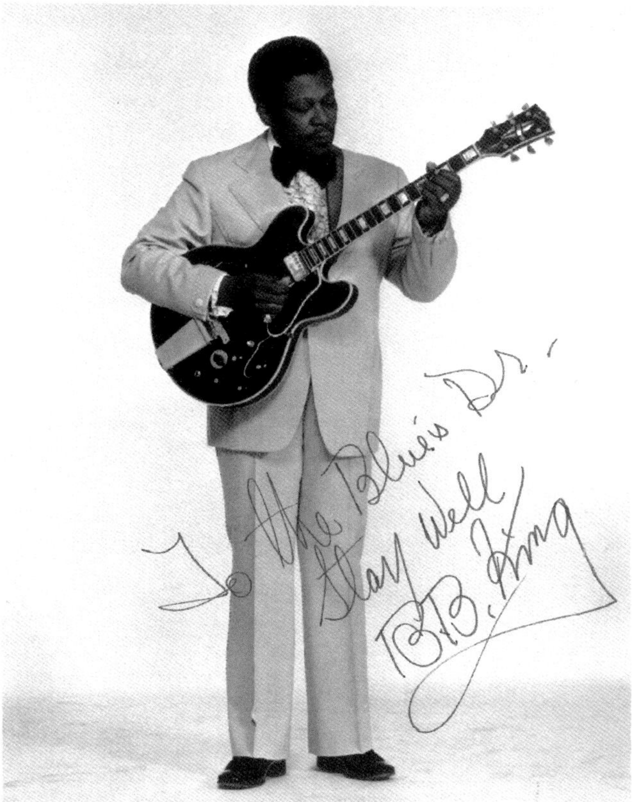


An autographed picture from B.B. King. *Courtesy of Drink Small, personal collection.*

title song of his album *I'm Tired Now*]. Now I'm so sick, what else I'm gonna do?...Old people know...Gotta talk to Lord now."

Instead of Drink attending the senior center for medical care and socialization, Drina arranged for a visiting nurse and Meals on Wheels to come to the house. Drina explained to friends who expressed concern about Drink, "You gotta just give him some time to go through what he's going through. He'll be all right in a few weeks. I tell Drink he needs to stop feeling so sorry for himself, saying, 'God is punishing him.' God ain't punishing him—God saved him! I tell him there are people with nothing, nothing from the waist down, and they're not complaining. He's just a little disabled. Complaining? No! I don't want to hear it."

Later that June, B.B. King played the Township Auditorium in Columbia. Drink heard how the older musician struggled with the performance from others who attended:

*B.B. King, he eighty-seven, man can't pat his foot…Got about five hundred people working. You'd be surprised—doctors, nurses and the band, publicist, secretary and accountants. He's a big organization, hundreds of people working on his staff. See, I'm just a lil freelancer…Al Green, ten- or twelve-piece band, got four or five guys over here dancing, doing choreography, got four or five people singing, got two or three keyboard players, tambourine player…production. Now look at how television shows go, all the producers, designers, might be about thirty names…It take all that to make a production…What happens, it cost $60,000 to get B.B. King. He got his bus, he got a band bus…On his bus he got the guard, the driver, the nurse—he got everything on there.*

*He did a commercial for diabetes…See that big money, you getting big money, see, you can't be sick. Like a guy got a football player, making $20 million a year. The guy, a manager that might have hired him, might get $100 million, just pay him $20 million. They got a big insurance on him…go get hurt, they patch him up, out a play. Man, I'll bet that man hurtin' almost cryin'. That man paying him $20 million a year, you better not be sick.*

As Drink began to physically feel better, his mood became better, just as Andrina had predicted. He refocused on getting his voice back in shape so he would be ready for the award ceremony, and he enjoyed receiving the congratulatory messages from fans across the country posted on the Facebook page set up by his friend Clair DeLune. The week before the event, after exploring every possible option, Drink was not sure he would have a way to get to Memphis. So it was agreed that Drink, Drina and I would make a road trip to Memphis. We departed Columbia at one o'clock in the afternoon on July 30.

Although Drink has never driven a car, he knows the roads of South Carolina better than most. The fact that he could not see made no difference at all. Drink was an excellent back-seat driver and gave directions while he and Andrina exchanged colorful and amusing banter and stories along the way. We took time to record the entire trip, just as if Drink were making a personal travelogue video for his friends and fans:

*I love y'all, and I'm on my way to knock 'em out in Tennessee…Well, I was born in 1933. It took a long time to play at this lifetime achievement in Memphis, have mercy* [laugh]*…I been to a lot of places, but nothing like this, Mem-phis* [laugh]. *Tell everybody in South Carolina I love 'em.*

> *I'm going to Memphis, Tennessee. Me and my guitar, Geraldine, we gonna raise hell in Memphis!* [laugh] *Drink Small love all of y'all.*

Drink continued to give directions: "Where are we now?...All right, you going the right way, jus' keep going. Stay on 20." It was a long drive, and at one point Drina said, "Let me know when you want me to drive." As if on cue, Drink spoke up from the back seat: "You can't drive. No, you can't drive to Memphis." Drina disagreed: "I drive every day. I drive to work, don't I?" Drink was not convinced: "That ain't the same thing. You can't say jus' 'cause you drive around town a little bit...That's not the same thing as highway driving!" Drina leaned over and whispered, "Jus' 'cause one time I was driving and I was tired and, well, I guess I kinda swerved a little bit." She was whispering, but he heard her and shouted back, "Where's my ID? You got my ID, Andrina?" Andrina shot her response back: "You're not driving; why you need your ID?" Drink shot right back to her: "If you drive and wreck the car, I wanna make sure I got my ID on me. I want them to be able to identify my body!" Andrina and I laughed, and I chose to continue to do the driving. Drink continued with the directions. "Where are we?... Tallapoosa. Stay on 20; you gonna see Talladega...Okay, where are we now? You gotta get on 78 soon; you see 78? Don't stay on 20, you gonna end up in Louisiana."

Time passed, and Drink reminisced while Andrina and I listened to country music on the radio. Drink said:

> *Drina and I were at a club. A friend was playing, so we were there. Made me so mad—you remember that, Andrina? This guy was drinking, drinking a lot, I could tell. Andrina was talking to some other people at the table. This guy takes his guitar, goes up to sing. Now this supposed to be a friend of mine. I hear him singing, "Look, look, look over there y'all, see that nappy-headed gal with the hunchback Drink Small." If I could, I would have knocked him out. That thing, that made me mad. And he was supposed to be a friend...I've had the blues four times: black-baby, black-child, black-man and now black–old man. Each one start out the same.*

We rode in silence for about hour. It was almost 9:00 p.m. when we crossed into Tennessee. There was something beautiful about the darkening night sky, the distant flashes of lightning and the Tennessee mountains as we pulled into the welcome center. Drina was trying to convince Drink to get out of the car for a few minutes and stretch his

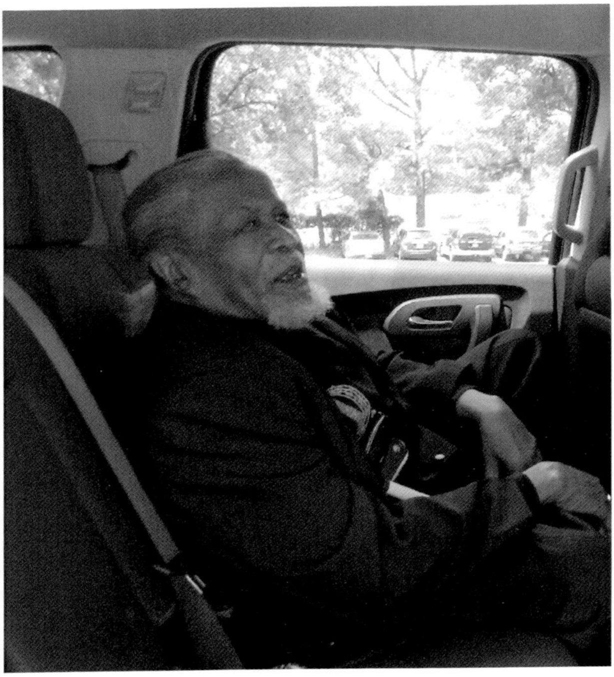

*Left*: Drink riding to the 2013 Jus' Blues Music Foundation award ceremony. *Courtesy of Elfi Hacker.*

*Below*: Big Llou Johnson, the "Voice of B.B. King's Bluesville" Sirius XM radio, greets Drink Small at the 2013 Jus' Blues Music Foundation award ceremony in Memphis, Tennessee. *Courtesy of Elfi Hacker.*

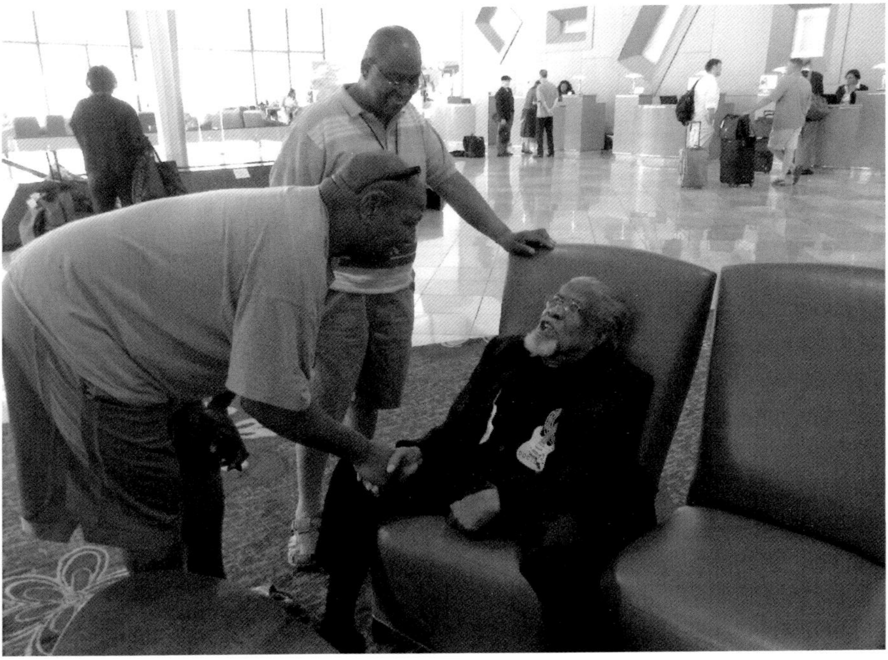

legs. He had eaten practically nothing at all the entire trip and didn't want to drink anything either. Drink agreed to walk the eight feet up the ramp and sit on a picnic bench. As Drina described the beautiful scenery, he only said, "I wish I could see it." A few minutes later, we were back in the car.

We arrived in Memphis at about 10:00 p.m. It had been a long ride. The next morning, we made another travelogue video. Drink said, "This is Drink Small. I'm leaving now, coming to the Hilton for the interview… Feeling good, I'm feeling good. It been a long time coming, a change gonna come."

Drink was wearing his black shirt with white hand-stitched details of a guitar and intricate lettering. While seated in the lobby of the hotel, Drink suddenly became moody and irritable. He was obviously irritated once again that he could not see what was happening.

> *Bad is negative. No matter how you figure, it's negative. You got a bad man, bad wife, bad condition, bad health, it's bad. You can't have a lifetime achievement two times. A person can't have two lifetimes unless one's in heaven. Lifetime and you got nothing to show—that's a dead life. Even a bullfrog got a life. I thought I was done in '92; I wasn't blind then. I got a good reason to sit on my behind now. I'm fixing to hang it up. I mean it. I thought I was getting ready to leave here last time.*

The conversation was cut short as Big Llou Johnson, the announcer of B.B. King's Bluesville satellite radio station, stopped by to introduce himself to Drink Small.

Almost immediately, people started coming up to Drink to shake his hand, ask for his autograph and take pictures. A reporter from *Living Blues Magazine* who had covered Drink on numerous occasions stopped over to discuss another possible feature. As friends came up to reconnect with Drink, it was obvious that they were not aware that his eyesight was partially gone. Old friends would extend their hands and then appear puzzled when he failed to shake them. I heard another say, "What's up, man, don't you recognize me?"

Elfi Hacker and her daughter Charlotte arrived at the Hilton lobby around 1:00 p.m. The devoted Winnsboro club owner and friend had driven all night and arrived in Memphis at about 4:00 a.m. Drink was appreciative and happy to see her. "Elfi, you feelin' healthy," he laughed. Cassie Fox from Whitmire, South Carolina, came into the hotel with her husband. The hotel

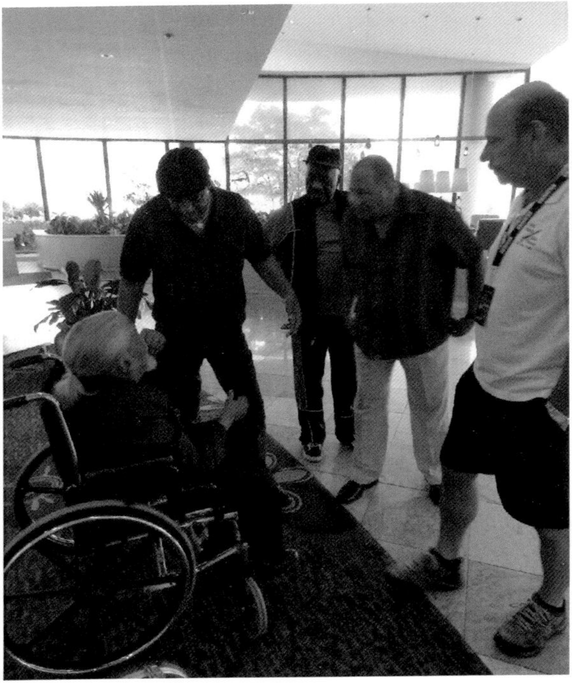

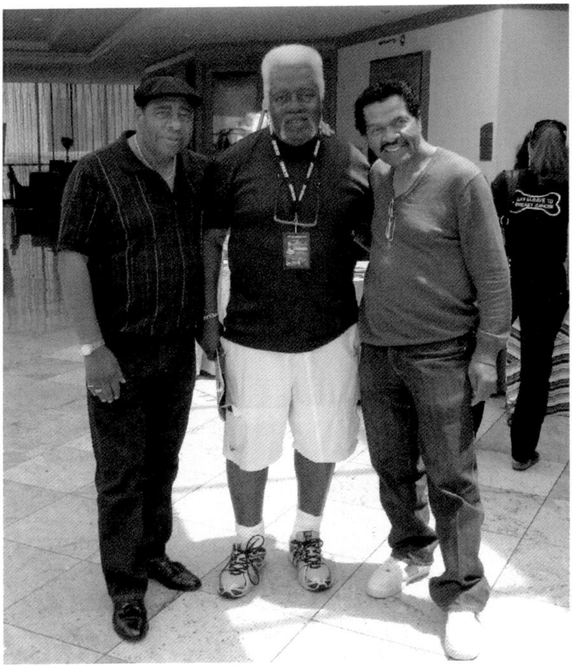

*Top*: Drink greeting fans at the 2013 Jus' Blues Music Foundation award ceremony. *Courtesy of Elfi Hacker.*

*Left*: Benjamin "Benny" Lattimore (center) with fans at the 2013 Jus' Blues Music Foundation award ceremony. *Courtesy of Elfi Hacker.*

*Opposite, top*: Andrina helps Drink prepare for the 2013 Jus' Blues Music Foundation award ceremony. *Courtesy of Elfi Hacker.*

*Opposite, bottom*: Drink posing at the 2013 Jus' Blues Music Foundation award ceremony. *Courtesy of Elfi Hacker.*

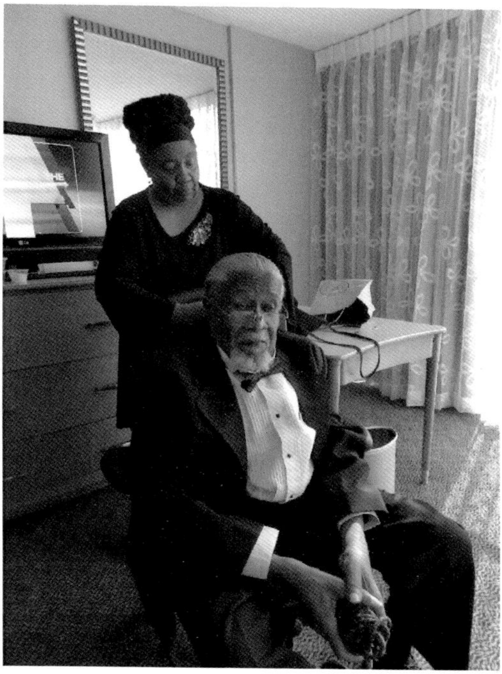

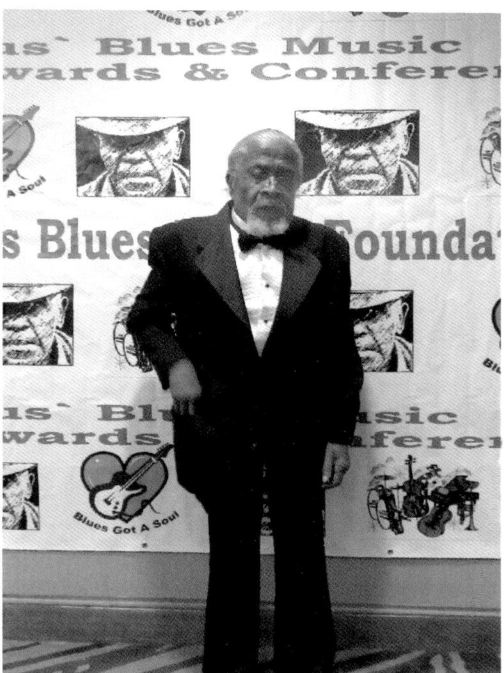


lobby was getting crowded. Drink had been sitting quietly in a chair for three hours. Drina was getting frustrated and set out to find the event director. She returned to inform us that due to the number of people checking in and those commuting from the overflow hotel, the press conference would be combined with the evening's award ceremony at 6:00 p.m.

Drink was finally given a room to rest. By 5:30 p.m., everyone was refreshed and ready to head down to the main event. Drink was now wearing a tuxedo, his silver hair neatly brushed back in a ponytail. He agreed to ride in a wheelchair down the elevator, and we agreed that once he got off the elevator, we would ditch the wheelchair, allowing him the dignity of making his entrance with Drina on his arm.

The little entourage moved out of the room together. Just past the lobby was a life-sized bronze statue of W.C. Handy, father of the blues. Behind the statue was an architectural water wall that slowly changed from green to blue to red. We guided Drink over to the statue and posed for a picture. Slowly, his fingers moved across the bronze likeness, over Handy's

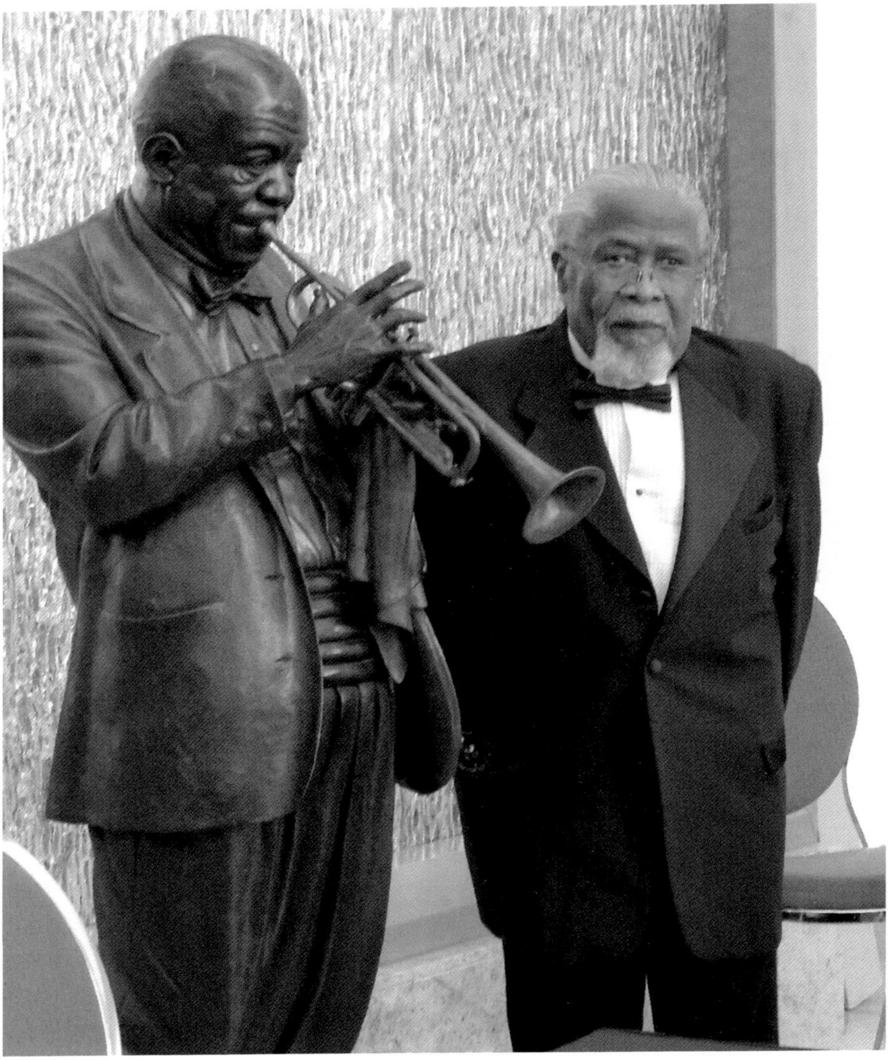

Drink Small and the statue of W.C. Handy in the lobby of the Memphis Hilton. *Courtesy of Elfi Hacker.*

fingers, on top of the cornet, up to the lips, nose and eyes. He whispered, "This is him. This is the father of the blues."

It was late when Drink was finally summoned up to the front to receive his lifetime achievement award. He graciously accepted the plaque, and then he kissed it. Other awards were given, and a few more speeches were made. It was almost an hour later before Drink Small was brought back up front to demonstrate before the audience why he was the newly appointed ambassador to the blues.

Drink was seated at the mic. He had his guitar, and the fire engine red strap stood out against his white tuxedo shirt. He did some quick bantering with the audience, and then out came the slide. His voice was incredibly strong, and his fingers were strumming, then sliding and then slapping the strings of the guitar. His voice stretched from octave to octave. The crowd was on their feet as he led them in a call and response of "Little Red Rooster":

*I got a little red rooster*
*(Little red rooster)*
*I got a little red rooster*
*(Little red rooster)*
*Oh yeah, oh yeah, yeah, yeah*
*ooh-wee-ee-eeee—lil red rooster—ooh-weeee*

While the crowd continued to clap and the lights were still dim, Drink sat back in the wheelchair and we left the ballroom. He was tired and just wanted to go home. To make him more comfortable, we agreed to make a bed in the rear of the SUV. A friend helped walk Drink to the car. He was still wearing his tuxedo as he perched on the tailgate, sliding backward into the vehicle until he was able to pull his legs inside and lay down. Drina got in the front seat, and we set the navigation and headed out of Memphis. It was 10:00 p.m.

By 9:30 a.m., we were entering Columbia. We were tired, but the loving banter between Drink and Drina continued. Drina called back to Drink, "Drink Small, you want something to eat?" He spoke for the first time since we left Memphis: "Yeah, I guess you can get me something if you want to." Drink was shifting around in the back of the car as we got in line for the drive-through. His ponytail had come loose, and he had his jacket half off. As we pulled up to the window, Drina laughed: "Lay down, Drink Small. That girl see you from the window, she might call the police. It must look like we kidnapped you, grown man in a tuxedo, trapped in the back of the car, last seen going through the drive-through at Bojangles!"

After arriving at the house and unloading the car, Drink finally appeared to relax. He used his white cane to make his way up the walkway and into his living room and sat in a chair. Drink sat, exhausted, holding his award. The

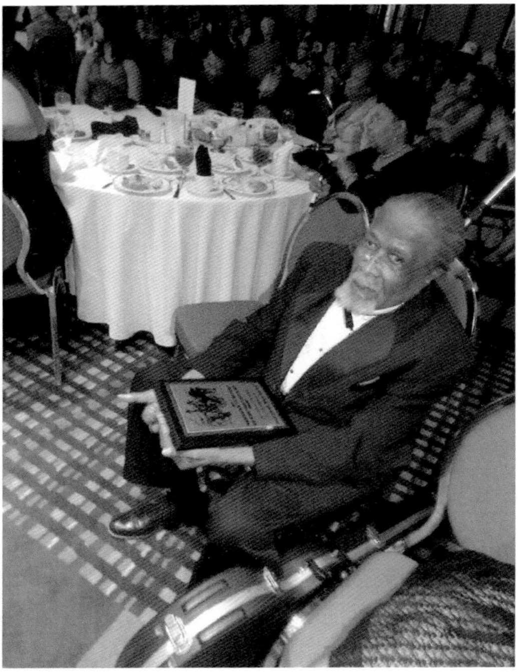

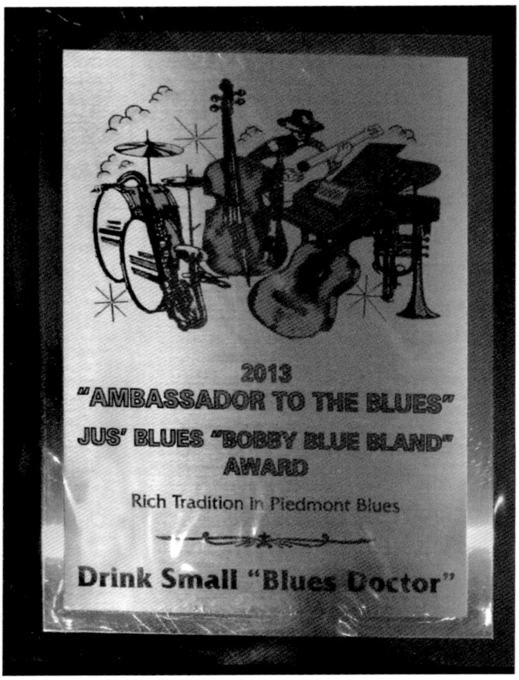


*Top*: Drink Small seated in the ballroom of the Memphis Hilton, holding his award at the 2013 Jus' Blues Music Foundation award ceremony. *Courtesy of Elfi Hacker.*

*Left*: The Jus' Blues Bobby Blue Bland Ambassador to the Blues Award. *Courtesy of Elfi Hacker.*

*Opposite*: Drink and one of his Geraldine guitars, 1999. *Courtesy of Cassie J. Fox (CazFox-Fowler) Photos.*

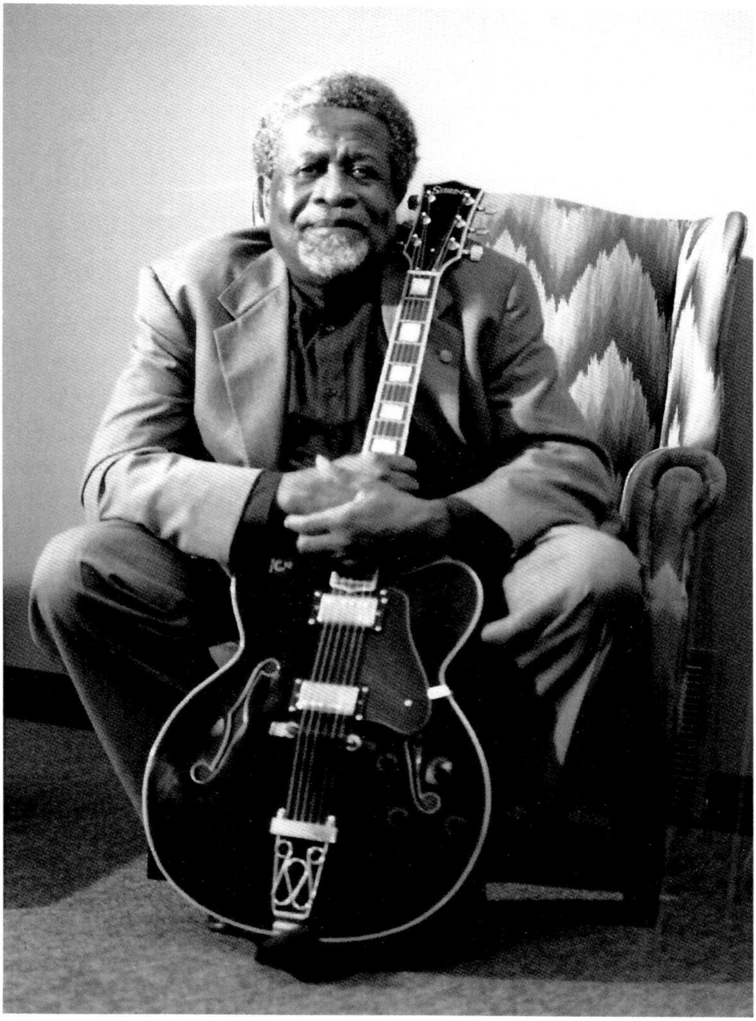

award is a plaque not unlike the dozens of plaques and certificates that cover every inch of the walls in the small house. Drink sat caressing the plaque like it was the most valuable thing he owned. In one last interview for our Columbia-to-Memphis travelogue, I asked how he felt about receiving this particular lifetime achievement award. He smiled and, in a soft voice, said:

> *It was great. It was wonderful, and I thank all the South Carolinians—that's my home state, where I was bred and born. And I won't leave,*

*'cause I'm trying to keep my roots in the state where I was born. And I probably could have grown more than I have, but I love my South Carolinians...I'm just like Fat's Domino* [laugh]. *He never left New Orleans* [laugh], *and me, I never, ever gonna leave my home. This is my home, my South Carolina.*

*I want to say something, something to y'all.*
*I want to say something, I want to say thing to y'all.*
*You ain't gonna hear the Piedmont blues played right*
*Until you hear Drink Small.*
*I want to say something, something to all of y'all*
*A lot of 'em want to play it, and a lot of 'em really try.*
*A lot of 'em really want to play it so, and a lot of 'em really try.*
*You might think you doing it real*
*But I'm gonna prove to you, you ain't doing it right.*
*I don't blame a man for trying to do the best he can*
*I don't blame a man for doing the best he can.*
*When it come down to Piedmont blues*
*You know Drink Small is the man.*
*I wanna holler! But the town too small.*
*You know I want holler y'all, but the town too small.*
*Y'all hear the Piedmont blues*
*You gotta hear Drink Small.*

# *Chapter 6*
# DISCOGRAPHY, DRINKISMS, LYRICS, LETTERS AND MORE

## DISCOGRAPHY

*The breadth of Drink Small's repertoire is fascinating in itself, but what's even more impressive is his depth as a performer in any of his chosen genres. His records may suddenly shift from a solo acoustic blues guitar track to a smooth soul ballad with horns to who knows what, yet Small never seems to be caught out of place. He can be gruff and rough, clean and modern or light and bouncy, altering his voice and guitar to suit the mood. Rated one of America's top gospel guitarists before he turned to blues in the late '50s, the South Carolina "Blues Doctor" for years had only one 45 on the market (Sharp, 1959). His discography has recently begun to grow considerably, finally revealing the extent of his songwriting and performing talents.*
—*Jim O'Neal, co-founder* Living Blues *magazine*

2008: *Tryin' to Survive at 75* (CD, Bishopville)
2006: *Blues Doctor: Live & Outrageous!* (CD, Erwin Music; originally released in 1990; available in Europe through Crosscut Distribution, Bremen, Germany)
2003: *Drink Small Does It All* (CD, Bishopville; out of print)
2003: *Considerable Grace: The Music of the South Carolina Folk Heritage Awards*—track #13 by Drink Small (CD)
2002: *South Carolina's Shared Traditions: 15 Years of the Jean Laney Harris Folk Heritage Awards*—track #7 by Drink Small, 1990 FHA Recipient (CD)

1994: *Electric Blues Doctor Live* (CD, Mapleshade)
1991: *Round Two* (LP, cassette, CD, Ichiban; out of print)
1990: *The Blues Doctor* (LP, cassette, CD, Ichiban; out of print)
1989: *Drink Small Live at the New Orleans Jazz Festival* (cassette, Bishopville; out of print)
1988: *Blues Doctor: Live & Outrageous* (cassette)
1987: "I'm Gonna Shag My Blues Away" b/w "I'm in Love with a Grandma" (45 rpm, Bishopville; out of print)
1975: "Atlanta, Georgia, Is a Little New York," Parts 1 & 2 (45 rpm, Bishopville; out of print)
1959: "I Love You, Alberta" b/w "Cold, Cold Rain" (45 rpm, Sharp #101; out of print); Drink also says he cut two more sides for Sharp that were never released: "Irene Goodnight" and "Rock 'n' Roll March." Where are the masters? It is another one of the great mysteries of the blues.
1957: "Pressing On" b/w "Family Prayer" (with the Spiritualaires of Columbia, 45 rpm, Vee Jay #847; Drink Small on guitar)
1956: "Can't Hide Sinner" b/w "When the Saints Go Marching In" (with the Spiritualaires of Columbia, 45 rpm, Vee Jay #181, out of print; Drink Small played guitar and sang bass)
1956: "I'm Going on to Glory" b/w "I'm Out on Life's Ocean" (with the Spiritualaires of Columbia, 45 rpm, Vee Jay #210, out of print; Drink Small played guitar)

Drink Small also played on three 45s by fellow South Carolina artist Kip Anderson: "I Want to Be the Only One" b/w "The Home Fire Is Brighter After Awhile" (Sharp, 1959; Drink Small on guitar); "I Done You Wrong" b/w "That's When the Crying Begins" (1964, Drink Small on electric bass); "Jesus Sings With Me (Lorna, 1982; Drink Small on guitar).

*I Know My Blues Are Different Because I'm the One Who Has 'Em* (LP, reissued on CD in 2002; Southland, available elsewhere, 1972)
"Bowlegged Woman"/"You Can Call Me Country"/"Can't Kill Nothing"/"My Baby Loves Me Right"/"My Rod"/"Hangover Blues"/"Corn Whiskey"/"Ugly Woman Blues"/"Worth a Million Dollars"/"If My Luck Don't Change"/"Liquor and Women"/"A Sad Time"/"You Make Me Feel So Good"/"One Woman Is Enough for Me"

*The Blues Doctor*
1990 (Ichiban)
"Tittie Man"/"Little Red Rooster"/"So Bad"/"Something in the Milk Ain't Clean"/"Rub My Belly, Baby"/"Leave Your Panties Home"/"Stormy Monday Blues"/"I'm Going to Move to the Outskirts of Town"/"John Henry Ford"

*Round Two*
1991 (Wild Dog/Ichiban Blues series)
"DUI"/"Steal Away"/"Thank You, Pretty Baby"/"Don't Let Nobody Know"/"Widow Woman"/"I'm Tired Now"/"Honky Tonk"/"They Can't Make Me Hate You"/"Bishopville Women"/"Can I Come Over Tonight?"

*Electric Blues Doctor Live*
March 1994 (Mapleshade)
"Stormy Monday"/"I Feel Good"/"Three O'Clock in the Morning"/"The Things I Used to Do I Don't Do 'Em No More"/"I Really Don't Want to Know"/"Charleston Women"/Instrumental/"I'm in Love with a Grandma"/"Shout"

*Drink Small Does It All*
June 2003 (Bishopville)
"I Want to Make Love"/"You Don't Have to Be Funky"/"Fish Fryin' Momma"/"A Woman Is the Sweetest Thing God Ever Made"/"Bingo Lover"/"Mr. Green Is the Barbecue Man"/"South Carolina Boogie"/"You Can't Take the Country Out of Me"/"Coon Shine Baby"/"Plain Old Country Blues"/"Come on Let Me Love You"/"You Got to Love Everybody in the World"/"Glory, Glory"/"Motherless Child"/"I'm Gonna Run On"/"Roll, Jordan, Roll"

*Blues Doctor: Live and Outrageous!*
May 2006 (Erwin)
"Swing Low, Sweet Chariot"/"Glory Hallelujah"/"Charleston Women Blues"/"I Really Don't Want to Know"/"I Feel Good"/"Little Red Rooster"/"Thank You, Pretty Baby"/"I Stand Accused"/"Shout"/"The Twist"/"Stormy Monday Blues"

*Tryin' to Survive at 75*
May 2008 (Bishopville)
"Bishopville Is My Hometown"/"Drink Small Boogie"/"When You Tell One Lie, You Gotta Tell Another"/"Do What the Lord Say Do"/"The Lord Been Good to Me"/"Three River Blues"/"Never Too Late to Do Right"/"Don't Bump My Stacy Adams Shoes"/"Tryin' to Survive at 75"/"The Righteous Will Always Win"

## *Singles*

"I'm Going to Shag My Blues Away"
1987 (Bishopville)

"The United States Will Never Be the Same" (Parts 1 and 2), tribute to Barack Obama
2009 (Juke Joint)

"Living in a Barbeque World"
September 2011 (Bishopville)

The story of Drink Small has truly allowed me to come full circle. After recently learning about the book, a young man who works for the same organization as I do in Little Rock, Arkansas, e-mailed to say:

> *Last night I was on Drink Small's Facebook page and found the new article highlighting him in* Columbia Living *magazine. I did not realize you were the same Gail who was quoted in the article, but when I searched for the book I went to your Kickstarter page and knew exactly who the author was!*
>
> *I'm glad to know you're writing the official Drink Small bio. I can't believe we never talked about him during Summer Academy* [City Year, Boston, Massachusetts], *considering his was the epitome of my guitar-hero guitar-slinging years in high school. He signed my guitar back in 2007 and told me to "keep the blues train rolling." I saw him for the first time at the Camden Blues festival in 2006, then again at Cumberland's in Charleston in 2007, and the last time I saw him was at the Blind Tiger in Charleston when I was in college.*
>
> *—Ross Scarborough, City Year, Little Rock*

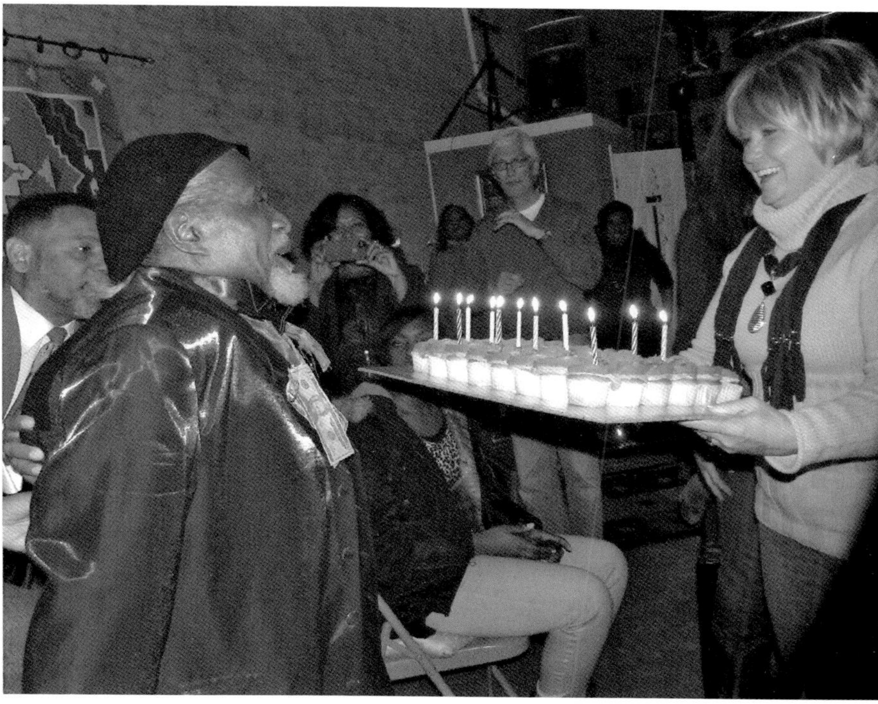

Cheryl Hartness holds the cake and Drink blows out the candles at his eighty-first birthday party at the 145 Club. *Courtesy of Elfi Hacker.*

On a visit to his home, Drink and I were sitting on the couch just finishing up an interview session, enjoying a cola, and I wondered, in that moment, if he was given one wish, if he could wave a magic wand, what would he wish for? International fame? Wealth or perhaps his eyesight? I thought this was as good a time as any to find out, and so I asked him.

GWG: Drink, let's say you're walking along the beach. You got your sandals on, wearing a pair of Bermuda shorts… [I'm working hard to set the scene by using my very best "once-upon-a-time" voice. I continue.] All of a sudden, out of the water washes up a mysterious bottle. It lands right at your feet. [I pause a moment and glance over to see if he is playing along with me in what I consider to be a very creative little game.]

DS: Uh-huh, I'm listening.

GWG: [I continue the story a little faster for dramatic effect.] You reach down and pick up the bottle, start to rub the dirt and sand off of it and BOOM [I wave my hands in the air], out pops a genie. He says, "Your wish is my command." What would you wish for, Drink? Tell me, what would you wish?

DS: [Slowing, Drink picks up the story with a few clarifying questions.] You say I'm walking along the beach?

GWG: Yes, that's right.

DS: …And an old bottle washes up out the water?

GWG: That's exactly right, yes, go on.

DS: [Drinks starts spinning a yarn faster than I can catch up, giving me a complete dramatization with gestures and images of his own.] What you think I'm gonna wish for? Here I am just walking long the beach, picking up the bottle, maybe put it close to my nose, and what you say? BOOM! That thing could break my nose off! BOOM?! Like that? Help me, Holy Ghost! I'm already blind, now I could lose my nose. Oh no, Lord, what? You trying to kill me? I'd start to run for my life! And then you say what? A big old what? A genie? Shoot—gonna what? Jump out the bottle? Oh no—it could, that thing…could be another…Lizard Man!

[By now, I am laughing so hard I can't talk. We are both just a' howlin' and laughing, and he keeps going.]

DS: Yeah, that could be Lizard Man number two! And you said it goes BOOM?! I tell you what I wish, BOOM? That could be one of them terrorist genies!

[We both start laughing again.]

DS: I wish? I wish you go ahead and throw that ol' bottle back out in the ocean, that's what I wish!

## Drinkisms

The Drinkisms listed below are attributed to Drink Small:

- The way you do Drinkism? Take some of my knowledge, some of my wisdom, put a little rhythm and you got the Drinkism. Yes sir.

- I got a bootleg life. My history is so messed up it's crossed. When you don't know who all your sisters and brothers are, that's a bootleg life, like my music, and that's a bootleg answer.

- Picking cotton wear you out.

- "Pray for me"—now that's a request, and it could be a noun and it could be a verb. Depends on how I use it…It's good way to start.
- Got church people that know me from church and never heard me play blues guitar, got blues folk that know me from the club they ain't never been inside the church. And me, I love them both the same.
- Blues wore me out, and there is no substitute for something that's worn out.
- Ain't no shame in my game, ain't no nervous in my service and that's it.
- Blessings are to give. If I had a million dollars, I'd give away 90 percent and keep 10 percent for myself, for me and Drina.
- Being with me will drive you crazy.
- I'm like a hound dog 'cause I got a lot to say.
- Home is not a juke joint and it ain't a church.
- All my ideas are good; you just need to figure out how to organize 'em.
- I gave all I had.
- You got ten dollars and you lose it all. I got twenty dollars and lose all that. Somebody else may have fifty dollars and lose it too. We all just lost everything we had.
- Negro spiritual is a true song, start you crying…"God bless the chile that got his own"…Now that's the truth.
- I ain't got a lot of education, but I got a lot of dedication.
- Everything can educate.
- Don't bring me any flowers. No, don't do it. I'm superstitious.
- I'm a folklorist, doin' it and ain't gettin paid.

- You lose your only son, it can't figure right. So sad you wanna cry.
- I'm a poor man, so I got the blues twice.
- Everyone need help sometimes. Car only need four tires, but it got a spare.
- I can understand why people commit suicide…They think, "What am I living for?" When you can't pay the bills.
- Vacation? I ain't never had one.
- How do you smile and play the blues? You got to have the blues in your bones.
- I got a big mouth, like a bigmouth bass.
- You gotta listen to the negative to get the positive.
- If it had not been for the Old Testament, there wouldn't have been a New Testament.
- Music not a thing I took up. It a thing in me.
- You hear me play gospel, the blues come out. You hear me play blues, the gospel come out. If you good, they both sound good.
- You can't live without the blues. A lot a people got the blues confused.
- You can't get around the blues—you can't get around 'em.
- I got a big head. I'm loaded with philosophy. I'm gonna write a book. It gonna be a hard book to write. I'm gonna call it *Me, Myself and I.*
- I'm an old rapper. I been rapping all my life. Now I'm fixing to wrap it up.
- I got enough things on there to be a billionaire, yes, sir, but this an ordinary.

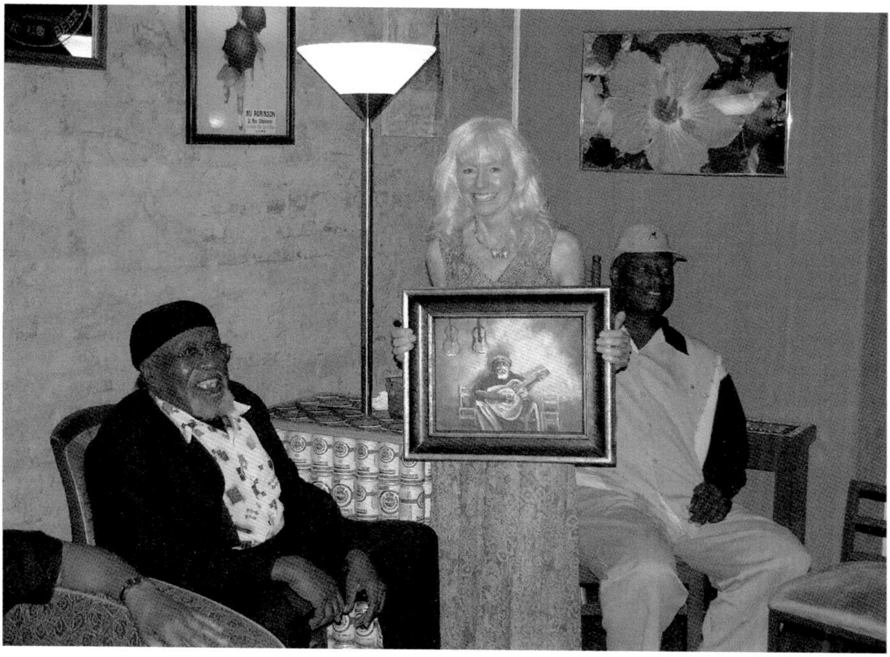

Dr. Janet Lynne "J.D." Douglass holds a portrait of Drink at the 145 Club. *Courtesy of Elfi Hacker.*

- I might be sick, but I can talk. I might look frail, but I still can wail.
- The poet in my talk—that makes the Drinkism.

## LYRICS

Drink was on his daybed reclined at a sharp angle, propped up slightly by a few pillows to support his upper back. The television, radio and tape player were all on at the same time. He uses the different sounds to help guide him from one room to another. Drink, wearing a black sweatshirt and light gray sweatpants, as he frequently does, was holding his large black office-style desk phone on his left knee. We talked as the music from one of his CDs continued to play from the boombox on the tall bookshelf in the corner. His long, slender fingers curled around the top of the phone poised to

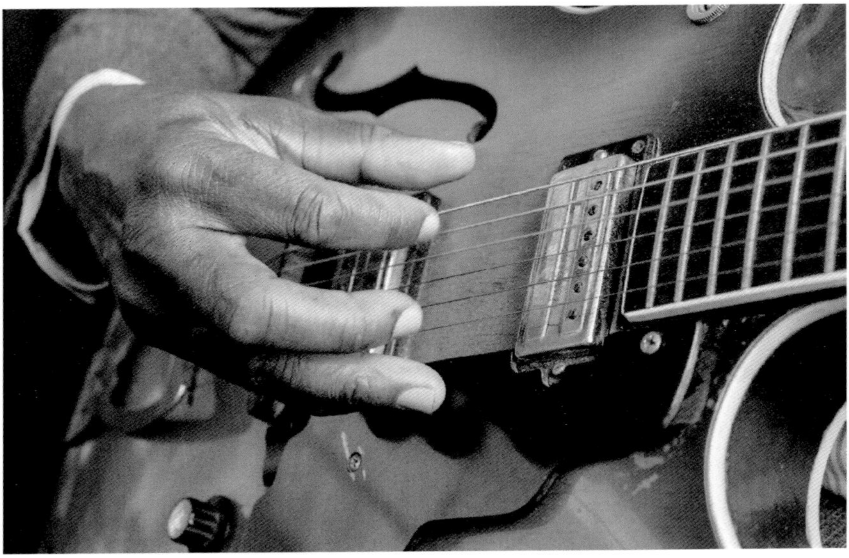

February 18, 1990 feature story by Elizabeth Lealand, Bob Leverone photographer. *Courtesy of the* Charlotte Observer.

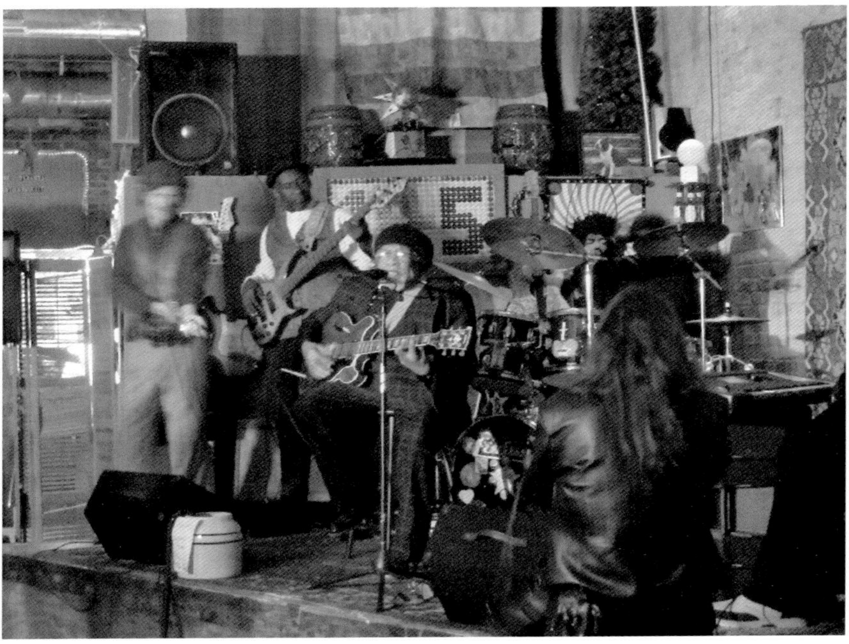

Drink playing at his eightieth birthday at the 145 Club. Clair DeLune is taking pictures. *Courtesy of Elfi Hacker.*

immediately lift the receiver. I noticed his wedding band seemed a bit too large. We had been talking about my recent interview with J.T. Anderson. Drink said, "He played with me a long time!" Suddenly, he was not listening to me at all; he was listening to his own music, intently. His eyes were fixed toward the ceiling; he was listening and waiting. Then came the guitar solo—his solo. His eyes shot to the left in the direction of the tape player and then back to the ceiling. As the guitar solo continued, I saw his lips, moving without a sound, eyes darting toward the boombox, back to the ceiling and he was smiling. Strangely, his eyes fluttered and blinked closed. That's when I heard the clicking sound. I looked down and saw Drink's fingers lifting, alternating quickly, pausing only to start tapping on the black phone once again as if strumming the guitar. For the next three minutes and fifty-four seconds, Drink Small was oblivious to the commercials on television, the radio playing in the next room or even my presence. He was physically, emotionally and spiritually consumed by the sound of his own guitar.

*"Slave to the blues"—Thomas Dorsey*

*Blues, please me do I have to die a slave?*
*Do you hear me pleadin', you gonna take me to my grave*
*I could break these chains and let my worried heart go free*
*If I could break these chains and let my worried heart go free*
*But it's too late now, the blues have made a slave of me.*

Like so many blues musicians of his era, Drink never wrote down his lyrics in a formal way. He would change the words at will and enjoyed creating new verses based on the venue he might be performing in at any given moment. The basic theme and overall melody was consistent; however, the song could be delivered in a hundred different ways. Drink's speech pattern and invention of words and phrases make transcribing his lyrics extremely challenging. For the purpose of this book, I wanted to transcribe a few of Drink's popular songs.

When discussing the transcription idea, he was insistent that I not include any of the risqué blues songs and said, "No, don't do that—I got grandkids. I don't want people to remember me like that. Please, I'm asking you—don't do it."

The following lyrics have been transcribed as Drink Small requested. Enjoy.

### "Bishopville Is My Hometown"

Bishopville my hometown. You know that where my ol' stomping ground
The houses where I used to live. They done tore 'em all down
That's in Bishopville, my hometown (I'm gonna do it again)
Bishopville my hometown. You know that were my old stomping down
The houses I used live down there. They done tore 'em all down
That's in Bishopville, my hometown
I was raised in the country. In a lil old shack
I moved to Columbia, South Carolina, and I didn't went back.
The houses where I used to live. They done tore 'em all down
That's in Bishopville, that my hometown.
Those days on the farm, never be forgotten.
I tried to crop tobacco. I couldn't pick no cotton.
The houses down there (Lord, Lord, Lord) where I used to live
(They done tore 'em all)
That in Bishopville, that my hometown.
You know down in Bishopville where I finish high school
You know that where I learned the golden rule.
The houses down there who-hoo. They tore 'em all down.
That's in Bishopville, my hometown.
I remember those days walking behind the plow
I look at my poor mamma, my mamma milking the cow
The houses where I used to live. They done tore 'em all down
That's in Bishopville, my hometown
I done played my guitar all over the world
Talking 'bout Bishopville, South Carolina, the place that I love.
The houses where I used to live. They done tore 'em all down
That's in Bishopville, my hometown.

### "Fish Fryin' Momma"

She's a fish fryin' momma and that's no doubt.
She's a fish fryin' momma and that's no doubt.
The way she fry it, it will melt in your mouth.
And if you taste it one time, you try it again.
And if you taste it once, you try again.
She fry the best fish sandwiches you ever stuck your teeth in.
Now yeah
(boogie-woogie piano)
Yeah, whoo.

**"Living in a Barbeque World"**
Believe it believe, believe it
Living in a barbeque world
Believe it, believe it
Living in a barbeque world
I been eating barbeque so long
It's hard for me to give it up.
A patient said to the doctor,
"Don't give me no bad news."
The doctor told me, "I hate to tell you,
But I got to take you off of barbeque." No
Living, I'm living, living in a barbeque world
I been eating barbeque so long it's
Hard for me give it up.
Patient came to the doctor
He say, "Doctor, I'm not gonna tell you no lie.
I eat barbeque every day of my life
And I'll eat it 'til the day I die."
'Cause I'm living, I'm living
Living in a barbeque world
I been eating barbeque so long
It's hard for me to give it up.
You know the old folks they love it.
And the young people love it too.
You can't find nobody in the United States
Don't like some kind of barbeque.
We're living, we're living, living in a barbeque world.
The preacher said to the congregation,
"I'm gonna tell something to you.
I got high blood pressure,
But I got to have my barbeque."
We're living, we're living
Living in a barbeque world.
I been eating barbeque so long
It's hard for me to give it up.
A lady say to another one,
"Honey, I'm a hundred and two.
I ain't got no teeth in my mouth, but I'm crazy bout barbeque."
We're living, we're living

Living in a barbeque world.
I been eating barbeque so long
It hard for me to give it up.

**"If You Tell One Lie"**
When you tell one lie you got to tell another, so quit lying.
If you tell seven lies 'cause first lie got to have a cover.
When you tell one lie you got to tell another
You got to tell seven lies because the first one got to have a cover.
Now suppose you tell me one thing
You tell another thing to someone else
And when the two of us get you together, you got yourself an awful mess.
When you tell one lie you got to tell another.
You got to tell seven lies, the first one got to have a cover.

**"I Love You, Alberta"**
I love you, Alberta, girl all by yourself
If I don't get to Alberta, I don't want nobody else.
Tell me, Alberta, whether you did me wrong.
Tell whether you did me wrong.
Alberta, tell me if you did me wrong.
You made me love you and you left me all alone.
You know the first time I met you held you in my arms.
You know the first time I met you I held you in my arms.
You know Alberta, girl, I was fascinated by your charm.
You know how Alberta I love you with all my heart and—Help me.
You know I love you with all my heart.
You know I really do, Alberta.
I love you with all my heart.

**"South Carolina Boogie"**
(Spoken) South Carolina boogie,
(Spoken) I want you to boogie 'til your pants fall down
South Carolina boogie
South Carolina boogie
South Carolina boogie
South Carolina boogie
I'm gonna do it again, y'all sing this time, I'm driving
South Carolina boogie

South Carolina boogie
South Carolina boogie
South Carolina boogie
You can go to Chattanooga but you won't hear the South Carolina boogie
(Spoken) You know South Carolina got different regions
(Spoken) Peedee area and the Midlands and the Piedmont area
(Spoken) And Drink Small love 'em all
(Spoken) So I come down to South Carolina and
I boogie in the bottom
I boogie in the middle
And I boogie in the high point.
South Carolina boogie
South Carolina boogie
South Carolina
South Carolina boogie
You can go to Chattanooga but you won't hear the South Carolina boogie.

**"The Nurse Song"**
God has blessed me, blessed me to have a nurse
Because a nurse, she knows, knows when a man is hurt.
Before she go to work
She make sure my food is done.
She goes and she takes a shower,
Then she put that nurse uniform on.
And I look at her, I say,
"God has blessed me, blessed me to have a nurse."
Because a nurse she knows, knows when a man is hurt
She may not be no doctor
But she's kind as she can be.
She always knows when something is wrong with me.
God has blessed me, blessed me to have a nurse
Because a nurse, she knows, knows when a man is hurt.
Sometimes I'm kind of slow, slow getting out of my bed.
She comes over and hug me and say,
"Honey, let me rub your big head."
God has blessed me, blessed me to have a nurse
Because a nurse, she knows, knows when a man is hurt.
All you young men, take an old man's advice.
Now if you plan to get married, get a nurse to be your wife.

You'll say, "God has blessed you, blessed you to have a nurse
Because a nurse she knows, knows when a man is hurt."
Before she goes to work, she makes sure my food is done
And she goes and she takes a shower
And she put that that nurse uniform on.
And I look at her and I say,
"God has blessed me, blessed me to have a nurse
Because a nurse she knows, knows when a man is hurt."
She may not be a doctor, but she's kind as a woman can be.
She gotta be doggone good woman to put up with a man like me.
I can't believe it, God has blessed me, blessed me to have a nurse
Because a nurse, she knows, knows when a man is hurt.
All you young men, take an old man's advice.
If you plan to get married, get a nurse to be your wife.
God has blessed me, blessed me to have a nurse
Because a nurse she knows, knows when a man is hurt.
She may not be a doctor, but she's kind as a woman can be.
She gotta be doggone good woman to put up with a man like me.
God has blessed me, blessed me to have a nurse
Because a nurse she knows, knows when a man is hurt.
Help me, Holy Ghost, I know I gotta good woman.
I gotta say it again,
God has blessed me, blessed me to have a nurse
Because a nurse she knows, knows when a man is hurt.
Oh yeah eh eh

**"I'm Gonna Shag My Blues Away"**
I'm gonna shag, shag my blues away
I'm gonna shag, shag my blues away
I'm gonna shag my blues away if it takes both night and day
I'm invited to a shag party tonight
I'm gonna shag all night, if the beat is right
I'm gonna shag my blues away if it takes both night and day
There is something about that old shag music
Makes you feel so good, you gotta get on to your feet
I've got ants, I've got ants in my pants
I can't stand still, I gotta get up and dance
I'm gonna shag my blues away, if it takes both night and day
There is something about that old shag music

Makes you feel so good, you gotta get on to your feet
I've got ants, I've got ants in my pants
I can't stand still, I gotta get up and dance
I'm gonna shag my blues away, if it takes both night and day
I'm gonna shag my blues away, if it takes both night and day
One more time…
I'm gonna shag my blues away, if it takes both night and day

**"SOMETHING IN THE MILK AIN'T CLEAN"**
Yea baby, something in the milk ain't clean.
Went out last night to visit your friend
It's six o'clock in the morning, woman
You just coming in.
I don't ask you where you been, something in the milk ain't clean.
Your friend keep calling to take you to play bingo
And when you came home, baby,
A man kissin' and walking you to the door.
I don't ask you where you been.
Something you doing, baby, I know it ain't right.
What you do in the dark, baby, one day will come to light.
I ain't got to ask you where you been
I know something in the milk ain't clean.
You know I'm gettin', baby, I'm gettin' a rotten deal.
You can't fool me, baby,
Because I have played the field.
I ask you where you been
To know something in the milk ain't clean.
You know I can tell when my woman is cutting out.
If I was like some men, I'd put my fist in some man's mouth.
But I don't ask you where you been
But I know, something in the milk ain't clean.
You know I can tell, baby, when you are cutting out.
If I was like some men I know, I'd wanna punch someone in the mouth.
But I don't ask you where you been.
You better stick around, stick around for somebody else.
Let me call it, baby, call it what it is.
I don't ask you where you been
But something in the milk ain't clean.

**"I'm in Love with a Grandma"**

I'm in love with a grandma, she got grandchildren large as me.
I'm in love with a grandma, she has grandchildren large as me.
Even though she's a grandma, she's just as sweet as she can be.
Making love to a grandma sometime it make you wonder.
She say, "Don't worry about my age, Drink Small,
Age ain't nothing but a number."
I'm in love with a grandma, she has grandchildren large as me.
Although she's a grandma, she's just as sweet as she can be.
Grandma talking on the phone, grandchild snatched.
Grandma say to the grandchild, "Shut up—you talking to a younger man."
I'm in love with a grandma, she got grandchildren large as me.
Although she's a grandma, she just as sweet as she can be.
Grandmama get her check to the supermarket and get it cash.
She know I drink a little beer sometime.
She bring me back a six-pack.
I'm in love with a grandma, she has grandchildren large as me.
Although she's a grandma, she's just as sweet as she can be.

**"Too Much Water (You Don't Have to Be Funky)"**

There's too, too much water, too much water you don't have to be funky
Goin', goin' 'round, goin' around smellin' like a donkey [laugh]
One more time [laugh]
Too, too much, too much water, you don't have to be funky
Fanning all over me, smelling like a donkey
You buy a bar of soap (they come in fifty cents)
You don't have to smell like a Billy goat
Too, too much water, too much water you don't have to be funky
Goin', goin' 'round here, goin' 'round smelling like a monkey [laugh]
You be shame of yourself
Go down to the mental hospital—you need some help
There's too too too much water, too much water you don't have to be funky
Goin', goin' 'round here, you think you cool but you smelling like a mule [laugh]

**"Mr. Green Is the Barbeque Man"**

I want to tell y'all people something—anybody who love good barbeque
You come to Columbia, South Carolina, check out Mr. Green's
You might say to yourself, "I ain't got no teeth."

You go to Mr. Green's, a six-month baby could eat.
Now Mr. Green, that's the barbeque man, now Mr. Green, that's the barbeque man.
He cook it so well, you can't help but chew the skin.
I'm going do it for again Mr. Green.
Now Mr. Green, that's the barbeque man, now Mr. Green, that's the barbeque man.
He cook it so well, you almost can chew the skin.
Now Mr. Green cook the best barbeque in the town, now Mr. Green cook the best barbeque in the town.
And when you pass Mr. Green's place, you can't help but turn around.
Now Mr. Green, barbeque man, and that no doubt, he the barbeque man, Mr. Green.
And that no doubt. When you get some in your mouth, you can't help but pigging out.
Now Mr. Green, I wanna shake your hand, Mr. Green, I want to shake your hand.
I'll tell the world that you the barbeque man
One more time
Now Mr. Green, barbeque man and that no doubt, he the barbeque man, Mr. Green.
He cook it so well, you can't help but chew the skin.
One more time
Now Mr. Green, barbeque man and that no doubt, he the barbeque man, Mr. Green.
He cook it so well, you can't help but chew the skin.

### "Bishopville Women"

(Spoken) All right, here's a song about the women in my hometown—Bishopville women
(humming) Uh umm, mmm, mmm. Uh mmm, mmm mmm. Ah-hmm, Ah-hum, ah humm
(spelling) B-i-s-h-o-p. V-i-l-l-e
Spell Bishopville, baby, that is home for me.
That is home for me.
Uhmm, uh
Ain't no other women be any finer. All the pretty women down there
Prettiest in South Carolina.
Them Bishopville women, they sure look fine to me.

(humming) Uh umm, mmm, mmm. Uh mmm, mmm, mmm. Ah-hmm, ah-hum, ah humm
Down in Bishopville, where I finished high school
All the girls love me down there, always call me cool.
Those Bishopville women, those Bishopville women
They sure look fine to me.
(humming) Uh umm, mmm, mmm. Uh mmm, mmm, mmm. Ah-hmm, ah-hum, ah humm
All the girls in Bishopville say I was real grown
Play the kind of blues turn the women on.
Those Bishopville women, those Bishopville women
They sure look fine to me.
(humming) Uh umm, mmm, mmm. Uh mmm, mmm, mmm. Ah-hmm, ah-hum, ah humm
Ain't no other women be any finer
All those pretty women down there—Bishopville, South Carolina.
Those Bishopville women
(humming) Uh umm, mmm, mmm. Uh mmm, mmm, mmm. Ah-hmm, ah-hum, ah hummt
Them Bishopville women, them Bishopville women
(humming) Uh umm, mmm, mmm. Uh mmm, mmm, mmm. Ah-hmm, ah-hum, ah humm

**"I'm Tired Now"**

I getting tired now
I been playing a guitar for a long time.
You know I'm getting tired now, you know I been playing the blues for a long time now.
If I don't soon make it I'm going back to South Carolina and I'm gonna sit back down on my behind.
I been playing my guitar, people, ever since I was a little biddy boy.
I was fooling around with a guitar while all my friends were shooting marbles and playing with toys.
If I don't soon make it I'm going back to South Carolina and sit back down on my behind.
You know I have made a lot of albums you know trying to get national attention
And seems like now, I'm going to be an old man living off a pension.
I'm getting tired now, let me tell you

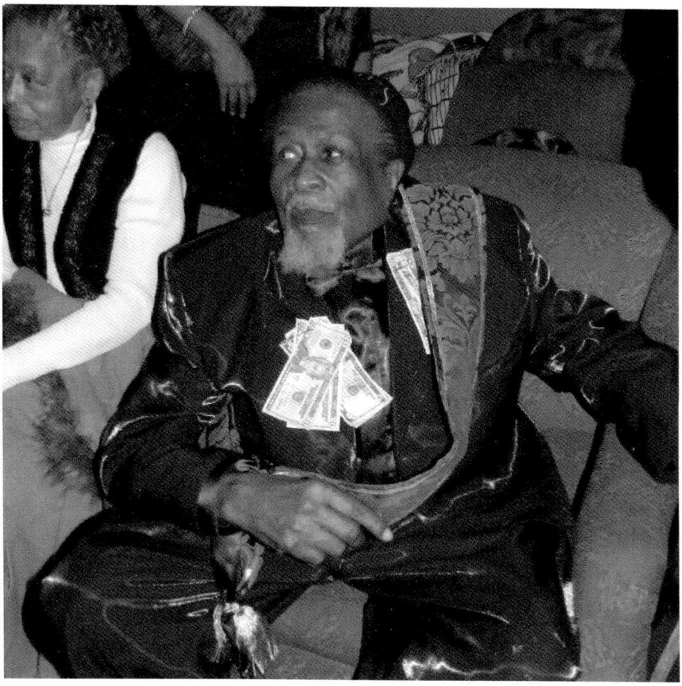

Drink's eighty-first birthday party at the 145 Club, wearing his CJ Martin-Marchese custom-made ambassador's sash. *Courtesy of Elfi Hacker.*

I been playing the guitar a long time.
If I don't soon make it I'm going back to South Carolina I'm gonna sit down on my behind.
You know I done played the blues, I played the blues everywhere, in Canada, at the Apollo Theater I also played twice at the World Fair
But I'm getting tired now, I ain't lying—uh ummm
Playing the blues for a long
You see if I don't hurry and make it, you know what I'm going to do
I'm going back to South Carolina, I'm going to sit on my behind.
Let me play the blues for you right now.
Yeah, you know I been playing the blues, if I don't make it this year you know what I'm going to do
I'm going home and play with my grandchild.
I'm getting tired now, I been playing the blues a long time.
If I don't hurry and make it, I'm going back to South Carolina I'm sit on my behind.
I'm tired now, tired now.

**"The United States Will Never Be the Same"**

Well, I wasn't able to make it to the inauguration ball
I wasn't there, I sit in the living room with the guitar every year
I wasn't there but my mind was there
Put your hands together y'all, put your hands together.
Come on.
The United States will never be the same. The United States will never be the same.
Been a long time coming, but it was the good Lord's plan that the forty-fourth president would be a black man.
The United States will never be the same.
Been a long time coming, but it was the good Lord's plan that the forty-fourth president would be a black man.
Black people, you need to jump up
Jump up and shout. They would laugh at us to see what you shouting about.
Now you can tell 'em what we shouting about.
Won't be very long before they shouting in the White House.
The United States will never be the same. The United States will never be the same.
Been a long time coming, but it was the good Lord's plan that the forty-fourth president to be a black man.
My mind go back to slavery times, see what the Lord did for us in 2009?
See, you just can't worry. You just got to wait. See, what he done for us nobody think about in 2008.
Now he's the Lord, he takes his own time. He gives us black president in 2009.
The United States will never be the same. The United States will never be the same.
Been a long time coming, but it was the good Lord's plan that the forty-fourth president would be a black man.
From the forty-third president, all of 'em were white. Lord sent the…down
He knew that wasn't right. Martin Luther King had a dream, see what it represents
I might not get there with you but…
The United States will never be the same. The United States will never be the same.
Been a long time coming, but it was the good Lord's plan that the forty-fourth president would be a black man.
All you black brothers pull up your pants, you might have a chance 'cause he be the president.

This also goes, go for the black and the white. I want all you people to try and get it right.
Stand hand in hand, stand with your brother, we gotta learn to love one another.
Now look here
I love Martin Luther King, I love Barack Obama.
I wish I had B.B. King with me. My guitar named Geraldine, B.B. King guitar named Lucille.
I take Geraldine, B.B. King take Lucille, we let the people know how we feel…
Put your hands together like you don't care, I don't care if you in your bed, you can at least nod your head.
One day, I'm gonna go to the White House, I'm gonna take my guitar and I'm gonna turn it out.
I want to shake Barack Obama hand, I'm Drink Small and I'm a bluesman
Oh yeah, Oh yeah, Oh yeah…

## Letters

*Dear Mr. Drink Small,*
*Hello, I heard it was your 80th birthday a few months ago. I thought I would send you a late birthday gift. Better late than never! I am a fan of your music and contacted Gary Erwin and he gave me your address. Hope you have a good year and wish you could make it to California to play some gigs! I saw you perform one time at Chicago Blues Festival…Maybe I will make it to the South Carolina festival next year. I also sent some photos, would you please autograph them for me? I enclosed a self-addressed and stamped envelope you can send them back to me in. Thanks so much and belated birthday wishes!!*
*Terry in California*

Drink Small has been nominated for numerous honors, including the National Heritage Fellowship. Rusty Sox, executive director of the South Carolina Arts Commission, has generously shared the following letters, which were submitted to the National Endowment for the Arts when it nominated Drink for the fellowship in 2011. These powerful testimonials demonstrate the continued depth and breadth of the legacy of Drink Small:

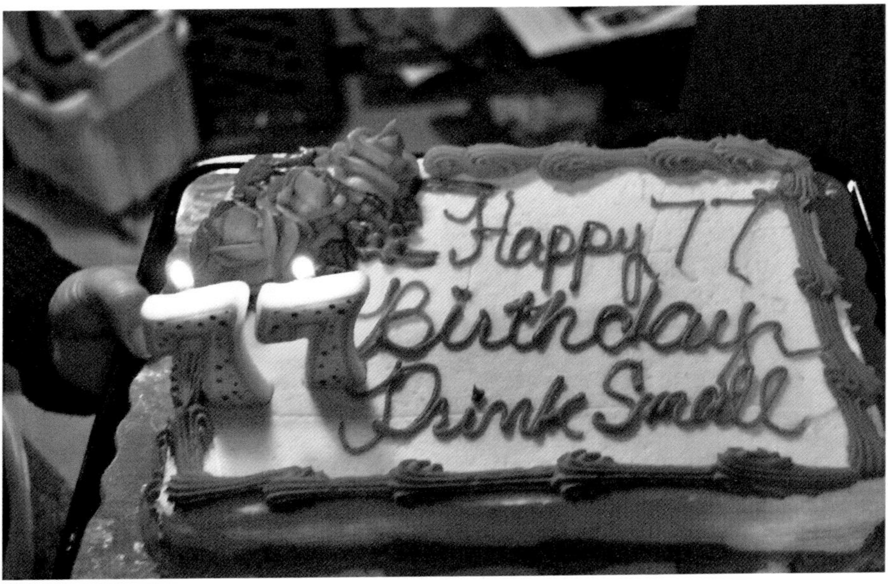


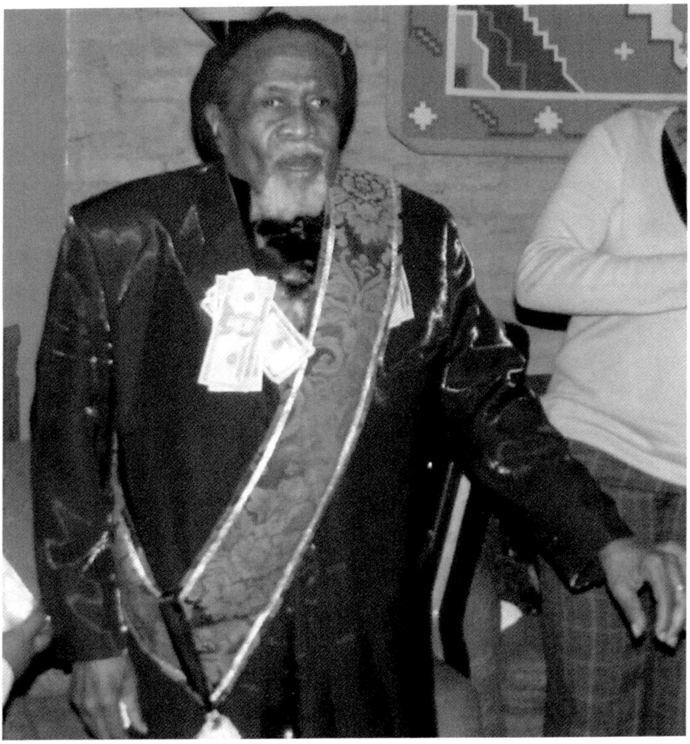

*Above*: Drink's seventy-seventh birthday cake at his 2010 birthday celebration at the 145 Club. *Courtesy of Elfi Hacker.*

*Left*: Drink celebrating his eighty-first birthday. *Courtesy of Elfi Hacker.*

*I am pleased to submit this letter of support on behalf of Drink Small. I have worked with countless traditional musicians during my tenure with South Arts and very few bring as much passion to their genre as Drink. What a timely nomination! He is a dedicated artist, gifted guitar player, unique vocalist, and above all, a true Bluesman. As long as I have known him, Small who is much more than simply a musician is, at heart and in practice, an educator who has shared his passion for the blues with audiences across the country.*

*What do I mean by "true Bluesman?" Small has built his repertoire on a life full of experiences—both good and bad. He has taken these experiences, folding them into song and commentary. The Blues to Drink is more than just a performance on a festival stage or in a juke joint or in a museum gallery. The Blues are about life—relationships, experiences, and how people treat one another. Small sings about people he has encountered, personal joys and hardship, love, hate, disappointment, victory, and everything that falls in between. Small sings to you as an individual, not at you. He imparts words of wisdom just as often in a simple conversation over the phone as in a performance on stage.*

*Small joined us for FITS 2007 (Folklorists in the South) in Ridgeland, South Carolina. His music was so enticing that the bride, groom, wedding party and their guests from a wedding occurring at the same conference space left their celebration and joined us for the evening. Small has that level of magnetism and openness of spirit.*

*South Carolina honored Small with the Jean Laney Harris Folk Heritage Award in 1990—the state's highest award for lifetime achievement in the traditional arts. That was 21 years ago! After receiving this "lifetime achievement" honor, Small has continued performing, writing, composing, touring—21 years after the award, and still counting. His tireless energy and mentorship to fellow musicians throughout the region is admirable and certainly earns him a place with the other master artists honored with a National Heritage Fellowship.*

*Sincerely,*
*Teresa Hollingsworth, Senior Program Director, South Arts*

*It is with special pleasure that I write in support of Drink Small's nomination for a National Heritage Fellowship. I can think of no artist more deserving of this honor. Mr. Small is an inspiration for fellow musicians and is recognized throughout the world as a living blues icon.*

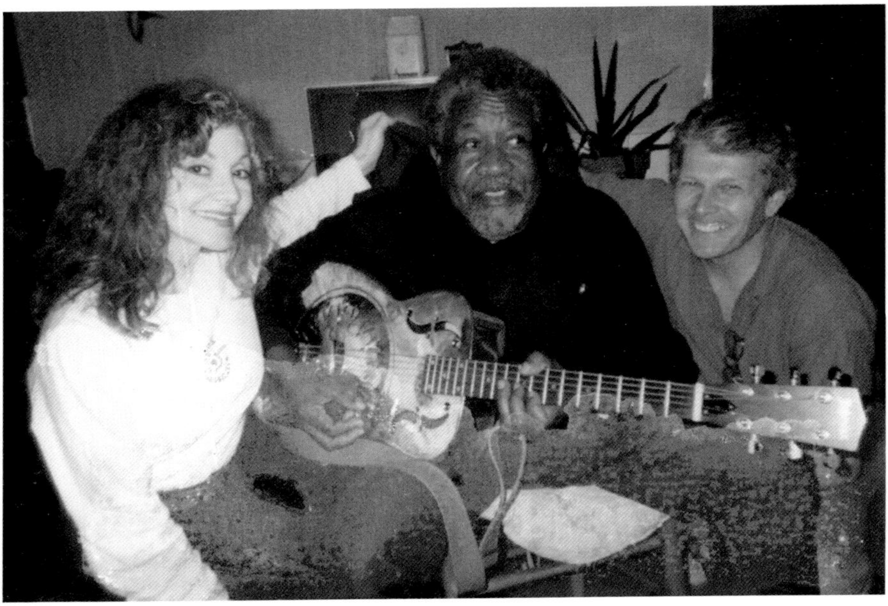

Country western singer Stella Parton (sister of Dolly Parton) visits Drink in his home before her December 2005 performance at the Newberry (South Carolina) Opera House. *Courtesy of Drink Small, personal collection.*

*From his early days on stage over sixty years ago to his performances for students on college campuses today, Mr. Small has been both an educator and an ambassador, as he has shared his passion for the blues.*

*Drink Small began his professional career in the 1950s with the gospel group The Spiritualaires, who recorded for Vee Jay Records, performed at the Apollo and Howard Theaters, and toured with the Staples Singers and Sam Cooke. The group received national acclaim as one of the best gospel groups in the country, and Small was named best gospel guitarist by* Metronome. *Later in the decade, Small played secular music and was influenced by a variety of styles, including the Piedmont and ragtime music of his own region. During the next five decades, Small toured the country and recorded over a dozen live and studio albums with music that ranges from blues, folk, and gospel standards to original rags and beach shags.*

*Like other great blues artists, Small draws on diverse influences to create a style that is distinctly his own. He learned from musical traditions in the community that surrounded him as a young man, he built on those traditions to create his own musical style. Small has toured the country as a gospel and blues musician for over half a century. He has played major American festivals, including the Chicago Blues Fest, the King Biscuit Festival, the New Orleans Jazz & Heritage Festival, the Smithsonian Folklife Festival—and internationally at the Finland Blues Festival. Small has also performed in venues that range from Lincoln Center and World Fairs to local juke joints.*

*Small embodies the very qualities that the National Heritage Fellowships celebrate. He is an artist whose contributions are dynamic and whose active practice has preserved historic blues repertoires. For half a century, Drink Small has performed and taught with a tireless passion that has earned him the admiration and respect of fellow musicians, scholars, and numerous students whom he has taken under his wing.*

*I enthusiastically support this nomination and can think of no artist more deserving of a National Heritage Fellowship than Drink Small. The Fellowship could not go to a more distinguished performer who represents such a distinctly rich blues heritage.*

Sincerely,<br>Bill William Ferris<br>Center for the Study of the American South

*Longevity, power, spirit and authenticity are some of the factors that have gone into the creation of the living legend that is Drink Small, The Blues Doctor. His background has been well-documented because he had the distinct advantage to come along during a time when musicians with his background were becoming revered and admired as holding the roots of American music in their hands—roots that grew into wondrous new music that changed the scope and face of music across the globe.*

*However, on the other hand, we have had a tendency to take American Blues Masters for granted; but, as they begin to leave us for the promised land more and more frequently, we find ourselves mostly left with artists who imitate, but cannot replicate the true Blues at its core. Drink is the genuine article, or as he might exclaim without an ounce of irony in his basso profundo voice, "Drink Small is the Real Deal!"*

*Drink Small is getting very close to his 80th birthday and still celebrates each and every day by playing and writing music, as he has done for over six decades. He is truly a living legend who inspires others, teaches values, entertains, and—as the Blues song says, "Loves the life he lives and lives the life he loves."*

*As the first professor of Blues History for the College of Music at the University of South Carolina and host of* The Blues Moon with Clair

DeLune *Blues and Roots Radio Show on WUSC-FM since 1990, it is an honor to be asked to present Drink Small for consideration for an Endowment for the Arts National Heritage Fellowship award. Drink has been South Carolina's Ambassador of Blues since long before I arrived in South Carolina 40 years ago.*

*From seeing him perform when I was a young college student to having Drink teach and play for my Blues History and Appreciation classes, to cheering him on as recipient of many awards, including the top state folklife honor, the Jean Laney Harris Folk Heritage Award, and being granted a key to the City of Columbia by Mayor Bob Coble, to seeing him perform recently at the Carolina Downhome Blues Festival in Camden, S.C., where he kept the early Saturday morning crowd enraptured, including recent National Heritage Fellowship recipient, Warner Williams. Williams arose early to hear and see Drink perform despite a late night the evening before, and sat raptly attentive through the entire performance. At the end, he asked for autographs and pictures of Drink. The admiration went both ways. As true fans of the other's work, it was clear that "excellence recognizes excellence."*

*Drink has been a constant inspiration for younger musicians and is truly a living Blues icon. From being brought up on stage five decades ago by the young Blues-Rock hawks of the day in the same way that the Rolling Stones revered Muddy Waters and Howlin' Wolf; to his modern day class performances for students who are just learning about roots music, Drink has been an educator and ambassador, spreading the love of this roots music that is truly American-born, but African inspired.*

*In one of the texts I used for my Blues History courses,* Encyclopedia of the Blues, *by Gérard Herzhaft, Paul Harris, Jerry Haussler, Anton J. Mikofsky, they compare Drink Small to Blind Boy Fuller and call his music "excellent for its mix of East Coast tradition mixed with modern sounds of Black music, country and Gospel."*

*Indeed, with the aging out of the population of early Blues singers, the true pentatonic sound has nearly disappeared from modern performers' styles. Blues has become less Afrocentric and much more Eurocentric. However, Drink Small—as he extols in one of his many wonderful CDs—truly "Does It All."*

*In the fashion of greats like Lead Belly, Drink is a "songster" but his style is unique and combines so many influences. He uncannily directs his performances to suit the audience. At a Blues in the Schools concert with Chicago Blues harmonica great, Billy Branch, Drink took a moment to educate the teens about the importance of paying attention to politics, then played a song he had written in honor of the first Black president, Barack Obama, which expressed his hope of being invited to play at the White House someday. Drink can play a quiet picnic or historic jubilee one minute yet rock the crowd at a large festival the next. In a nightclub setting, he might play some of his more risqué songs in his repertoire, but wisely discerns when to keep those off his playlist. His breadth is equal to his depth.*

*In an attachment to this letter, a folklorist for Berea College writes about Drink Small's style eloquently, and makes some apt comparisons with some of the top Blues names, such as Lightnin' Hopkins. Hopkins' visceral song, "Mojo Hand," evidences a similarity in playing style that goes back to the pentatonic rhythms that make roots music so distinct, even from Piedmont Blues, which Drink also plays expertly. Oddly, one of the reasons he is so adept is the same reason that many unschooled listeners erroneously critique Drink's work as being sloppy. African rhythms are based on five, not four, beats per measure and are often intentionally played ahead of or sometimes just behind the top of a note. That is what makes Drink's music genuine and unaffected by the modernity that has all but stifled the true roots sound. If you listen to Drink and Lightnin' you will hearken back to music of the griots, the African storyteller historians who carried the stories of the tribes down through time in their songs. These purveyors of oral tradition were honored long before there was a way to preserve them in written form.*

*Drink Small is one of the few authentic griots we have left in this country—sadly, when he and a few others are gone, there is scant chance of anyone rising to take their places; even the small numbers of those who honor the style through dedication and scholarly imitation, such as Roy Book Binder, Rory Block and John Hammond are becoming fewer and farther between and reflect, rather than originate.*

*In the chapter I submitted for the Novello Festival Press book* Making Notes: Music of the Carolinas, *Gary Erwin, who is a tireless supporter and promoter of Blues in the Southeast, was noted for his admiration of and support for Drink Small. Shortly after a well-attended birthday extravaganza that Erwin planned in honor of Drink's 78th birthday in January, 2011, which was held at the Bishopville Opera House in Drink's home town, Erwin said, "Drink Small's constant creative spark is amazing…he writes songs and stories every day and has been making it as a working musician for many years—through some meager times."*

*Honors such as this are among the many Drink has received. He has been the subject of* American Routes, *a public radio program hosted by Nick*

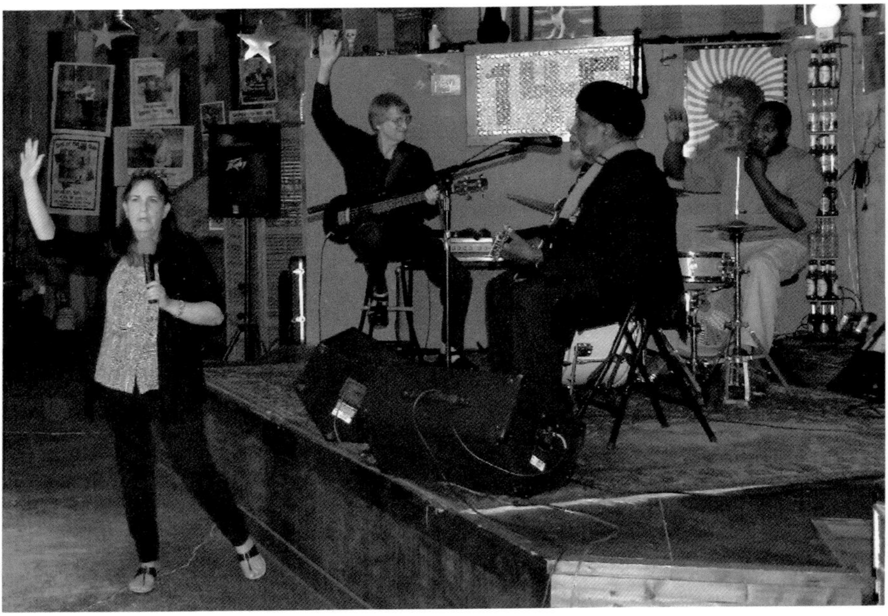

Clair DeLune, personal friend, blues "goddess" and host of *Blues Moon* radio, introduces Drink at his eightieth birthday party at the 145 Club. *Courtesy of Elfi Hacker.*

*Spitzer, and Juke Joints and Honky Tonk Legends, an S.C. Educational Television program that featured his music. He has been inducted to the South Carolina Music & Entertainment Hall of Fame and nominated for a W.C. Handy Award, which is given by the Blues Foundation in Memphis. Small's influence is not limited to his home state. He has performed at the Chicago Blues Fest, the King Biscuit Festival, twice at the New Orleans Jazz & Heritage Festival, and at two world fairs.*

*Last week, I traveled three hours across the state to hear him perform at the Franklin G. Burroughs/Simeon B. Chapin Art Museum in Myrtle Beach as one segment of a traveling exhibit called, "Story, Song and Image—A Collaborative Project of Painting and Music" by artist Glen Miller and music folklorist John Fowler. Watching and hearing Drink sing in front of a 10 foot folk-art painting of himself and his black dog is a visual and aural image that will last in my memory for life. South Carolina is extremely fortunate to have such a fine example of roots music and it is our hope that through this award, we can share this musical legend with the rest of the United States and beyond.*

*Drink Small's capacity to entertain, his amazing store of musical lore, his spirited and wry commentary and his staggering longevity, combined with his advancing age make now the perfect time to give the Blues Doctor a chance at being formally recognized as the national treasure we have long known he is.*

*It is with great pleasure that I nominate Drink Small for the National Endowment for the Arts' National Heritage Fellowship.*

*With deepest gratitude for your consideration,*

*Clair DeLune*
*Music historian, writer and professor*
*Producer and host of* Blues Moon Radio

# BIBLIOGRAPHY


All Music. "Arthur 'Guitar Boogie' Smith." www.allmusic.com/artist/arthur-guitar-boogie-smith-mn0000508600.

*American Historical Review* 21, no. 3 (April 1916): 504–27.

Anderson, J.T. Personal interview. August 16, 2013.

Bamberg Extension Annual Report, USDA War Board Report, January 5, 1943.

Billboard. "1957 Billboard Top 100 Songs." billboard.fm/charts/billboard/top-100-songs/1957.

Binkiewicz, Donna M. *Federalizing the Muse: United States Arts Policy and the National Endowment for the Arts, 1965–1980.* Chapel Hill: University of North Carolina Press, 2004.

Biography. "W.C. Handy." www.biography.com/people/wc-handy-39700.

Burke, K., and D. Griffin. *The Blue Moon Boys: The Story of Elvis Presley's Band.* Chicago: Chicago Review Press, 2006.

Burroughs, Jimmy. Personal interview. September 1, 2013.

Cassels, Rob. Personal interview. June 14, 2014.

Charles, Ray, and David Ritz. *Brother Ray: Ray Charles' Own Story.* Boston: Da Capo Press, 2004.

Columbia Yearbook for the S.C. Department of Agriculture, 1942, 1943.

Cromer, Tim. Personal interview. June 27, 2014.

DeBerry, Demetrius. Personal interview. August 9, 2013.

DeLune, Clair. "Drink Small the Blues Doctor." *Columbia Living* magazine, 2014. www.columbialivingmag.com/drink-small-the-blues-doctor.

Erwin, Gary. Personal interview. July 20, 2013.

Fox, Cassie. Personal interview. August 13, 2013.

Franklin, B.V. *Jazz & Blues Musicians of South Carolina.* Columbia: University of South Carolina Press, 2008.

Gass, Carrie. Personal interview. August 9, 2013.

Greenhaw, Wayne. *Woodcutters Organize: Echoes of Change in the South's Backwoods* 3, no. 1 (1980): 16–19, 22.

Guralnick, Peter. *Dream Boogie: The Triumph of Sam Cooke.* Boston: Back Bay Books/Little Brown and Company, 2005.

Hacker, Elfi. Personal interview. March 30, 2013.

Jackson, Vince. *The Littlejohn's Grill Story: Blues, Jazz, Rock and Roll in Clemson.* N.p.: Sugarcane, 2008.

Jones, Jacqueline. *Labor of Love, Labor of Sorrow: Black Women, Work and the Family from Slavery to the Present.* N.p.: Basic Books, 2010.

Lane, Annie Lou Moses. Personal Interview. August 9, 2013.

Maggin, D.L. Dizzy. *The Life and Times of John Birks Gillespie.* 1st ed. New York, 2005.

Manning, Edward, II. Personal interview. May 26, 2013.

Marshall, Edward O. *News and Courier,* July 25, 1986, 7.

McCuen, Sam. Personal interview. August 14, 2013.

Montgomery, E.S. *The Thoroughbred.* New York: Arco, 1973.

Perry, Scott. "Drink Small." www.scottperrymusician.com/2006/09/drink-small.

Rivers, Oscar. Personal interview. August 20, 2013.

Russell, Tony. "Bobby 'Blue' Bland obituary." *Guardian,* June 2013.

Sciway. "SC Historically Black Schools." www.sciway.net/afam/sc-historically-black-schools.html.

Secular Music Articles by Opal Louis Nations. opalnations.com/Articles.html.

Shrimp City Slim. www.shrimpcityslim.com/bio.html.

Simkins, Francis B. "The Ku Klux Klan in South Carolina, 1868–1871." Journal of Negro History 4 (1927): 606–47.

Small, Andrina Bratton. Personal interviews. February 2013–August 2014.

Small, Drink. Personal interviews. February 2013–August 2014.

Smith, Elaine M. "Bethune, Mary McLeod." In *Black Women in America: An Historical Encyclopedia.* Brooklyn, NY: Carlson Publishing Co., 1993.

Smith, Roland. Personal interview. August 9, 2013.

South Carolina African American History Calendar. "Drink Small." scafricanamerican.com/honorees/view/2002/9.

*South Carolina: A Handbook.* Prepared by the Department of Agriculture, Commerce and Industries and Clemson College. Columbia, SC, 1927.

South Carolina Department of Archives and History. "Columbia Township Auditorium." www.nationalregister.sc.gov/richland/S10817740134/.

———. "Dennis High School." www.nationalregister.sc.gov/lee/S10817731017.

Sumter County, South Carolina Largest Slaveholders from 1860 Slave Census Schedules and Surname Matches for African Americans on 1870 Census. Transcribed by Tom Blake, May 2001.

Underwood, Tut. "Drink Small: Prescription from the Blues Doctor." *Living Blues* magazine 104 (July–August 1992): 13–17.

Unknown Explorers. "SC Lizard Man." www.unknownexplorers.com/sclizardman.php.

Whiteis, David. "Drink Small." Chicago Reader. www.chicagoreader.com/chicago/drink-small/Content?oid=880734.

# INDEX

## G



## H



## J



## K



## L



## M



## N

## O



## P



## Q



## R



## S



## T

## U



## V



## W

# ABOUT THE AUTHOR

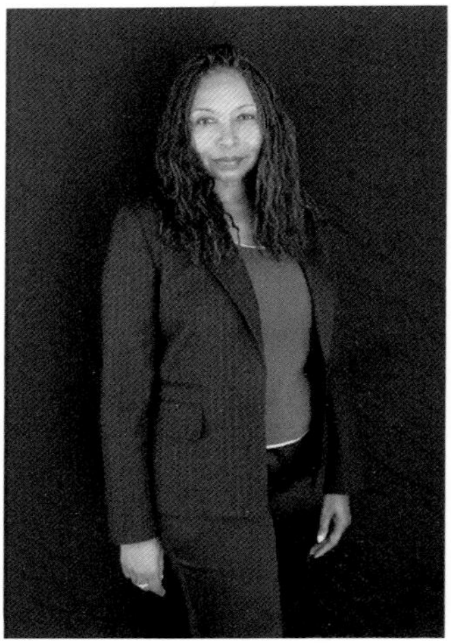

Gail Wilson-Giarratano is the executive director and vice-president of the education-focused nonprofit City Year in Columbia, South Carolina. She began her nonprofit career with the Lancaster Arts Council in Lancaster, South Carolina, and the Museum of York County in Rock Hill, South Carolina. As a former performing and teaching artist, she has worked for the South Carolina Arts Commission, the Caribbean Cultural Center in New York City and the Brooklyn Academy of Music in New York.

She holds a BA in art from Winthrop University, an MS in leadership and policy from Wheelock College in Boston and a PhD in leadership and decision sciences from Walden University. Her original one-woman show, *It's Cloudy in the West*, is based on family history and traces the life of a dance hall girl from a Carolina plantation to Dodge City, Kansas, in the 1800s. The play has been performed at colleges, schools, festivals and events throughout the East and was featured at the Smithsonian Institute in honor of Women's History Month. Gail currently resides in the Lake Carolina community of Columbia, South Carolina, with her blues musician husband, Anthony Charles (Giarratano), and their Great Dane, Adelina Bambina.